for Barbara Applegate, a Geriatric Care Manager

From Families Reaching Out for Help:

"This has completely upended all of us. Balancing everything, while also trying to still enjoy my mom has been crushingly overwhelming."

"Helping mom get paid services in place has been hard because she doesn't realize how much all the little things add up and weigh on the family."

"We are having a hard time establishing and maintaining boundaries. We tend to dodge the difficult conversations with her as well, like that she can easily afford a maid but wants the kids to come by and do everything. Or that she has ample funds to get a working iPhone so she can order her groceries and prescriptions to be delivered, but instead family overextends themselves taking mom on a lot of last minute, time-consuming errands."

"I still mourn the loss of my mother as an independent woman too. This has been the hardest trial I have ever endured."

"I do know that there are outside solutions to some of this, but my mom has not been open to much, so it's been slow going. In some cases, she'd rather go without, than pay for or even ask for outside help, and we're struggling to find the balance between honoring her wishes, and helping her realize that her quality of life could be so much better (and we wouldn't feel like such failures) if she'd be more open."

"I want to take her out to lunch, but I can't fit lunch in around the essentials that can't be overlooked."

From families who have been referred to Hospice:

"We appreciate your support, expertise and care you provided our family and our mom in our greatest time of need and grief."

"We couldn't have given our mom such a dignified and intimate end to her life without your team. We will never forget, and draw pride from the way we all worked together to fulfill her wish to stay in her home with her family."

"We will always be grateful."

A Compassionate Journey

The Definitive Guide to Providing Effective,

Loving Care for Your Aging Parent

Barbara Applegate, MSW, ACSW

Published by:
All Valley Publishing
Phoenix, Arizona

A Compassionate Journey:

The Definitive Guide to Providing Effective, Loving Care for Your Aging Parent

Published by:
All Valley Publishing
Phoenix, Arizona

Second Edition Copyright © 2024, Barbara Applegate, MSW, ACSW

All rights reserved. No part of this book may be reproduced or transmitted in any form or by any means, electronic or mechanical, including photocopying, recording, or by any information storage or retrieval system, without written permission by email or otherwise from the author or publisher.

ISBN 13: 978-1-960702-08-1

1 - Non-fiction   2 - Self-Help   3 - Healthcare   4 - Aging/Seniors

Cover Design: Freddy Solis
Editor: Donna Stark
Interior Design: Patti Hultstrand

Printed in the United State of America - Phoenix, Arizona

DEDICATION

To the adult children who want to understand
and offer the best care for their aging parent.

FOREWORD

When I first met Barbara Applegate over 20 years ago, she expressed to me that clients' needs were paramount and had to be fulfilled with integrity if I were to work with her in home care. During those early years, she impressed me with her advocacy for clients and the need to coordinate and collaborate with other professionals.

This was the first time I had collaborated with another business owner. Barbara trained me to think through the client experience and implement strategies that were effective. I've come to understand how concierge level service can be accomplished in adult home care. It's not "if" but "how" when it comes to care for clients.

I believe we have been able to provide care together at the highest levels over decades because of our shared value system. It's with great pride that I encourage any adult children seeking to help their parents or other loved ones through the aging process, to seek advice, counsel and wisdom in these pages.

In a time when service to others sometimes seems less than achievable, "*A Compassionate Journey: The Definitive Guide to Providing Effective, Loving Care for Your Aging Parent*" reflects her extensive knowledge and expertise in providing solutions and wisdom to those in need.

This comprehensive guide to parent care (or any elderly person) reflects Barbara's lifetime in Elder Care Advising. To Barbara, there are no shortcuts when it comes to in-home care.

With Gratitude,
Brent Owens
President & CEO
All Valley Premier Home Health Care

NAVIGATING THIS BOOK

Other Resource Documents & Full-Page Forms

All other resource documents and full-page versions of the forms and assessment questionnaires found in this book can be located at Amazon and on the books' website: *https://bestparentcare.com.*

Introduction

The first edition of "Parent Care – A Survival Guide for Adult Children of Aging Parents" was published in 1998. Since then, my team and I have had two additional decades of hands-on experience to offer in this updated workbook—including the unique challenges presented by the Pandemic Crisis of Covid-19.

I have been helping families navigate this maze of caregiving for over 40 years. Drawing upon my professional knowledge and experiences working with aging parents and their support systems - family, friends, and community, along with the support of the A.G.E. Consultants' Geriatric Care Management team of nurses, social workers, and psychologists - I hope that this workbook will guide you through your role as a caregiver.

For many of you, becoming involved or responsible for your aging parents' well-being is a new dimension in your relationship. Most likely, and at times, it will be confusing and difficult for both you and your parent.

Eldercare is always changing and as you participate in caring for your aging parent, you will develop a new awareness and skills to guide you forward in being a caregiver, both in the present and future.

Our healthcare industry has undergone a very intense period, resulting in numerous changes, including new infectious disease protocols and staffing shortages. With these changes in mind, this comprehensive workbook will be a dynamic tool to help you and your aging parent begin to plan for their long-term care.

Working through the first three chapters will provide you with the background information needed to make an informed decision about when and how to get involved in caring for your aging parents in the best way possible. Through questionnaires and assessments, you will gain a comprehensive understanding of your parent's current behaviors.

This workbook is designed to provide a thorough evaluation of the following key areas:

- Functional
- Mental and neurocognitive
- Psychological, social, and behavior
- Emotional and spiritual
- Suitable living arrangements

It is important to complete all the forms and questionnaires before you start planning for your parent's care. Be sure to involve your parent, family, friends, and professionals who are currently interacting with your parent to obtain a more comprehensive picture of your parent's needs. Once you review the data you have collected, you will be able to establish a realistic plan of care.

Other chapters in this book are designed to help you determine who and what are the best choices in the medical, legal, and financial areas to support your aging parent's needs. (Keep in mind that the information you collect will change as your parent progresses through their aging, so you need to remain aware of how and when these changes occur).

There is a chapter to raise awareness about the signs of elder abuse, equipping you with knowledge on how to watch for scams and safeguard against those who prey on the elderly, and a chapter that will guide you through the grief and loss associated with terminal illness. Eventually, your parent will also experience grief and loss as those around them pass away, or because they have to mentally and emotionally process the diagnosis of a terminal illness. There may be depression, or changes in their spirituality, so keep an eye out for those sides as well.

Finally, this book will address your needs as the caregiver of your aging parent. Generally, the person providing care is an elderly spouse who may also be frail, an adult child of an aging parent, or sometimes a relative or friend. Whoever it is, our goal is to help you consider what you may need to sustain your own health, well-being, and peace.

Caregiving is a demanding responsibility, often requiring significant time and effort. Some key points to think about are:

- Taking care of a frail parent can easily require more than 25 hours per week if they are still living in their own home.
- Many caregivers are called to care for both their parents and children simultaneously. This is called the 'sandwich generation'.
- The average number of years spent caring for a child is generally less than the number of years caring for an aging parent.
- It is our hope that as you go through the process of learning and caring for your aging parent you will also see the value of self-planning, and easing the burden on your loved ones as you also age.

Caring for an aging parent can be an overwhelming and life-changing experience, even in the best of circumstances. A sudden illness or fall can pull you and your family into a crisis of caring for your aging parent without the benefit of being prepared. However, it's also important to remember that you don't need an immediate crisis to decide if you should step in and begin care for your parent. There may be subtle signs that indicate it's time to become more informed about their evolving needs. Consider the following:

- Did your last visit with them go as you were expecting?
  - Were there changes in their behavior, appearance, or the nature of their conversation?
  - Did you see or sense that your parent is changing?
- Do you find yourself thinking about your parent more frequently?
  - Why? Are you worried? If so, about what?
- Was there a comment made about your parent that disturbs you?

- Who said it? What is their relationship to you and/or your aging parent? Were the comments of concern or criticism?

If there is a crisis or you simply have nagging doubt and worry about your parent, it is important to get involved and act. The questionnaires in this book will help you organize and prepare for the tasks and duties when your parent requires additional help or passes away, and the assessments are designed to help both you and your parent navigate the inevitable end-of-life. Using this workbook will help you stay focused and supported throughout this process. And don't forget, your needs are just as important as your aging parent's, so be sure to take the time for self-care. Proceed with caution, knowledge, compassion, patience, caring, and kindness - for both your aging parent and you.

How to Use This Book

The planning sections of this book and its forms are essential to the success of helping your parent get the most effective and efficient care possible. Chapters two, three, and four are those essential chapters. Once you assess the care they need, you can utilize the other information to carry out these action plans.

This process is not meant to be a one-and-done experience. As your parent's mental and physical health evolves, you'll need to re-evaluate their needs at least annually and adjust their care plan accordingly. You may even notice changes, thanks to the knowledge gained from this book, that you can now recognize as indicators that a reassessment is necessary sooner than the yearly mark.

Due to the need for continuous assessments, we have included full-page forms in a separate workbook for you to copy and use. We know this information is valuable in helping you with your parent's care. Please visit the book website (https://bestparentcare.com) before you start a new assessment process for any additional information or for updated contact lists and resources as they are added.

Staying on top of your parent's condition and proactively updating their care strategy is crucial for ensuring their well-being is supported over time. Moreover, we hope that as you go through the process of learning and caring for your aging parent, you will also recognize the value of self-planning, and easing the burden on your loved ones as you also age. Preparing for your own future needs can provide peace of mind for everyone involved.

1

Does My Parent Need Help?

IN THIS CHAPTER:

- **Real Stories: When It's Time to Evaluate Your Loved One**
- **Questions About Your Aging Parent**
- **Understanding Your Parent's Behavior: Impairment Signs**
- **Neurocognitive Disorders**
- **Alzheimer's Disease**
- **Types of Dementia**
- **Delirium**
- **Depression**
- **Your Parent's Emotional Needs**
- **Social Needs of Elderly Adults**
- **Psychological Needs of Elderly Adults**
- **Spirituality - What You Need to Know**
- **Emotional Health and Spirituality**

Real Stories: When It's Time to Evaluate Your Loved One

When I receive a call from a family, often their main concern is that their parent needs help, but they do not know how to proceed. For example, a frequent comment I receive is, "I've called my mother. She's not clear about who I am." Or their parent's neighbor has called them and has expressed concern about their parent and they want them to visit. There may also be situations where the parent has been hospitalized and will need more attention or care, or the hospital wants to discharge their parent but they have been told they cannot stay alone or they need help in their home to be safe. These are just a few of the many reasons why families are calling and looking for help.

Understandably, their first questions are, "Is that something you can do for me? Can you go in and see what's going on with my mother?" My response is, "Yes, but I will need some information first," and the first thing I ask is, "What are the actions that are concerning you?" Some of their concerns are: "Well, mom doesn't always answer my questions. Or she says what she thinks I'm asking her. And she's repeating a lot."

If family members are not local, we will offer to go out to do an assessment to see what the problems are. If they are local, we offer to meet them at their parent's home to evaluate what may be happening.

When we go out, we introduce ourselves and then explain that we are visiting them to assess their current situation and determine if any assistance might be required. Frequently, we will need to explain that their family is concerned and that we can help their family have peace of mind by evaluating the situation and determining if their parent does in fact need help.

A Brief Snapshot of Home Visits:

Upon arrival, we will observe and take notes on the environment and the parent. What do the living areas look like? Are they in disarray? Are the rooms clean, is the laundry or dishes piling up, or is there evidence of the parent not eating regularly? Does the parent look disheveled and is she/ he dressed appropriately? Does the house smell clean or are there odors suggesting a lack of proper hygiene or other underlying issues? Are there animals/pets that seem to be desperately in need of care?

Once we have been able to assess how the environment looks, we then sit and visit so we can ascertain if the parent is cognitively intact. In other words, if they can understand the questions being asked of them. I don't jump into a cognitive assessment immediately and I don't do a formal status exam at this point. I just ask, "How was yesterday? What did they eat? Are they feeling well or have they been able to take their medication?"

Once we have a better idea of how their parent is functioning, we can then help the family obtain a more complete assessment of needs and assist with developing a plan of action for them to follow.

Marie's Story: An Example of How We Can Help

I helped Marie since her family lived out of state. Marie was 96 years old and living alone. Marie had some local companions who provided 12-14 hours of weekly support.

We were concerned that Marie's living environment was not being adequately supported by her two companions. The refrigerator wasn't stocked properly, and she was pretty confused. We notified the family who lived in New York of this initial assessment.

We were able to get Marie evaluated and discovered that she was not making adequate or safe decisions. We invited the family to come to Arizona to work with her trust officer, financial advisor, and physician. We did a complete cognitive assessment and evaluated her independent activities of daily living. We also assisted her family in locating and organizing her important documents to make sure there was consistency and proper management of her personal affairs.

We developed a comprehensive plan of action and offered recommendations for the family to consider. Throughout all of this, the main aspects of Marie's life was discussed, including her deep attachment to her two caregivers.

Marie needed 24-hour care, but this was cost-prohibitive. We recommended placing Marie in an appropriate setting, which we helped with while the family was still in Arizona. Although the two companions couldn't meet Marie's care needs in her home, they still developed a strong emotional bond. To maintain that important connection in Marie's life, we also arranged for them to visit Marie twice a week.

The family had returned to New York knowing that there was a safe plan of care in place and that Marie was being cared for under the watchful eyes of her team, which included the financial advisor, her physician, a trust officer, and the Geriatric Care Manager.

Questions About Your Aging Parent

The hardest questions to answer about your aging parent are:

1. Is my parent managing to live safely without assistance?
2. Is my parent reacting to life circumstances adequately?
3. Are there signs or symptoms of a serious problem?
4. Is it time for me to get involved in managing my parent's day to day routines?

To effectively answer these questions, you need to recognize the critical signs and symptoms that indicate when it is time to become involved with your parent's routine activities.

This chapter will give you areas to consider as you observe your parent's behavior and will enable you to determine when and where they will need support. Reviewing a broad range of symptoms can help you identify how well your parent is managing day to day.

 You Cannot Do This Alone!

You will need the support of family, friends, and caregivers while gathering the information needed to complete the observations of your parent's routines and daily lifestyle.

Be sure to share what you and your support team have observed with your parent's physician and healthcare team. These observations of your parent's behavior in their home and community can greatly contribute to their overall care plan and treatment recommendations. This information also helps complete the picture of your parent's behaviors so his/her physician and specialists can develop an appropriate treatment and plan of action.

What You Need to Know

The information in this chapter is centered primarily on the illnesses and impairments that tend to affect elderly people and their ability to cope with living effectively and safely. These symptoms can appear singly or in combination and can present themselves either gradually or abruptly.

Keep in mind that many of the signs and symptoms of neurocognitive disorders (dementia), depression, delirium, and functional, emotional, spiritual, social, and behavioral disorders are all similar. Therefore, it is best to leave the diagnosis to your parent's physician.

Your first task is to understand what you need to know about the various illnesses and impairments that plague the elderly. Equipping yourself with this knowledge can help you assess the situation, identify potential problems, and determine how and when to get involved to help your aging parent.

According to the World Health Organization and the Geriatric Mental Health Foundation, the risk factors that can cause mental and neurocognitive disorders; functional, social, and behavioral dysfunctions; as well as emotional and spiritual problems are triggered by:

- Alcohol or substance abuse
- Loss of health or loved one
- Chronic illness (cancer, heart, lung, pain)
- Medication mismanagement (which may lead to delirium)
- Physical loss of mobility, strength, and/or endurance
- Depression
- Inadequate diet (malnutrition)
- Poor sleep habits

It is also very important to understand how isolation can take a toll on your aging parent's mental, cognitive, emotional, spiritual, and physical health.

When it comes down to it, older adults experience stress that goes along with aging, and that can become a risk factor for decline. A critical lesson learned from the Covid pandemic is how isolation can negatively impact our aging population.

Understanding Your Parent's Behavior: Impairment Signs

Signs of Impairments Fall Into Five Areas:

1. Functional Symptoms	Ability to manage self-care and daily lifestyle needs: personal care, transferring (i.e., needing help moving from a sitting or lying position to get from a bed to chair or toilet), nutrition, shopping, financial management, cooking, toileting.
2. Mental/Neurocognitive Symptoms	Primary features: memory, attention, language, learning, perceptions, thinking, understanding, communications, judgment.
Major Neurocognitive disorders **Please note:** the common term for Neurocognitive Disorders is **Dementia**: i.e., Alzheimer's dementia, Lewy Body dementia, Parkinson's dementia, Vascular dementia, and Frontotemporal dementia. *Throughout this workbook the term Dementia will be used when discussing these various Neurocognitive Disorders.*	General – not specific diagnosis but does include at least memory loss. In addition, other symptoms: loss of language skills, loss of judgment, loss of ability to perform executive skills, such as financial management, problem-solving, calculations, reasoning, learning new tasks or information, and understanding of one's relationship to time, place, and person.
Delirium	Acute confused mental state with sudden onset (within a few hours or days): disturbance in awareness, orientation and attention.
Depression	Mood disorder characterized by sadness, emptiness, or irritability often accompanied by physical or cognitive symptoms.
3. Emotional Symptoms	Feelings, attitudes, emotions, i.e., anger, hostility, frustration, sadness and loneliness.
4. Spiritual Needs	Meaning and purpose of life issues.

5. Social (social cognition) / Behavior Symptoms	Management of personal relationships, poor social judgments, impulsivity, personal neglect, Perception of others, decreased inhibition, less filter between thoughts, feelings and actions i.e., when acting angry, they are angry. When they are acting kind and happy, they are kind and happy. Decreases in social cognition offer a mirror to observe the inner feelings and thoughts of your parent. This can offer information that can be very telling of their unmet needs.
Behavior Symptoms: Driving-accidents, scrapes, damage to car or nearby objects: wall, trash cans, etc.	Driving can be dangerous due to the loss of skills- poor acuity, poor reflexes, poor judgment, poor perception of distance.
Use of Technology: cell phone, computer, etc.	Encourages Social interactions (both in-person and through technology —calling, texting, social media, etc.). Can eliminate isolation but can also create an opportunity for scammer and predators, so always be watchful and ask questions.

ACTION: Read through each of these areas
- Ask others in your parent's circle for their observations of any changing behavior.
- Discuss your impressions of your parent's ability to safely perform daily living needs with his or her physician.
- Request that a full geriatric assessment be conducted if you are seeing any changes in your parent's behaviors (signs of impairment).
  - Consider requesting a referral to a Neurologist, Neuropsychologist, Clinical psychologist specializing in Geriatrics, or a Geriatric Care Manager who will assist you in obtaining the appropriate specialists in Geriatrics.

What You Need to Know: Functional Status

Understanding your elderly parent's functional abilities will help you determine when and if you need to get involved in caring for your parent. An evaluation of their functional performance is essential for planning the necessary support.

Functional status refers to your parent's ability to perform tasks that are required for living independently and safely.

Areas of functional signs and symptom to observe:

- Does your parent have strong ambulation? Do they have a steady gait and good balance?
- Can your parent transfer themselves from a chair, toilet and into a car?
- Can your parent use the toilet without assistance
- Is your parent incontinent? Of Bladder? Of Bowels? Can they keep themselves dry and clean?
- Is your parent taking his/her medication properly? Are they remembering to do so?
- Can your parent manage meal planning, shopping and food preparations?
- Is your parent still driving? Are they a safe driver or do they have restrictions?
- Is your parent paying their own bills and managing his/her finances?
- Is your parent experiencing any changes in vision, hearing, smell, and touch?

Any cognitive or physical health changes can contribute to a decline in the ability to perform tasks necessary to live independently in their home or community.

You can acquire useful information about your aging parent's functional status by observing your parent as they complete simple tasks, such as unbuttoning and buttoning a shirt, picking up a pen and writing a sentence, taking off and putting on shoes, climbing up and down stairs, and getting up from the table, chair, bed, or toilet.

The Functional Assessment located in Chapter Two has two questionnaires that will help you determine if your parent has any signs or symptoms of impairment, and if so, what level of care will be needed.

The two questionnaires to assess your parent's functional ability are:
1) Activities of daily living (ADL)
   a. ADLs are self-care activities that a person performs daily (eating, dressing, bathing, transferring between the bed and a chair, using the toilet, controlling bladder and bowel functions).
2) Instrumental activities of daily living (IADL).
   a. IADLs are activities that are needed to live independently (doing housework, preparing meals, taking medications properly, managing finances, using a telephone).

ACTION:
- Once you have collected your observations be sure to review and fill in the Questionnaires in Chapter Two -Functional Assessment.
- At this point, it would be beneficial to consult with family members or caregivers actively involved in your parent's life to gauge their perspectives on the level of support and assistance your aging parent may require.
- Keep in mind this is a critical piece of information which will assist you in knowing what level of care your parent needs and how to best achieve this care.

What You Need to Know: Neurocognitive Disorders (Dementia)

Dementia is a very broad term used to identify signs and symptoms of mental impairments significant enough to interfere with a person's decision-making and safety.

- Important fact: Dementia can be confused with delirium or depression, so both need to be ruled out or treated before a diagnosis of dementia can be made.

- It is important to know that depression and dementia can co-exist.

There is a cluster of symptoms that can signal potential problems and should be assessed by a healthcare professional, such as a primary care physician or neurologist.

- Memory loss
- Complex attention (difficulty focusing)
- Loss of language skills
- Loss of judgment
- Loss of ability to perform executive skills, such as financial management, problem-solving, calculations, reasoning, and learning new tasks or information
- Loss of understanding of one's relationship to time, place, and person
- Changes in perceptual and motor functions
- Breakdown of filters between thoughts, feelings, and actions that are not socially acceptable

Facts:
Here is a touch of reality…you and your aging parent(s) are not alone!

- 5.7 million individuals are living with Alzheimer's and it is projected that 14 million individuals will have Alzheimer's Dementia by 2050.
- Every 65 seconds in the United States someone develops this disease.
- For every person with neurocognitive disorder in a nursing home, there are another two or three persons with an equal level of impairment being cared for in the community by some combination of family members, friends, and paid caregivers.[1]

---

[1] Geoffrey Tremont, "Family caregiving in dementia," U.S. National Library of Medicine (Med Health RI, February 2011). https://www.ncbi.nlm.nih.gov/pmc/articles/PMC3487163/.

Remember, dementia is a very general term for memory loss combined with the other symptoms that are severe enough to interfere with daily life. Forms of dementia include:

- Alzheimer's (the most common type)
- Lewy Body Dementia (the second most diagnosed)
- Parkinson's Disease Dementia
- Vascular Dementia
- Frontotemporal Dementia

Since other medical issues can cause dementia symptoms, it's important to get a good physical assessment from your aging parent's physician. Here is a list of examples that can present with symptoms that look like dementia:

- A subdural hematoma, cerebrovascular disease, or brain tumor.
- Certain systemic conditions such as hypothyroidism, severe urinary tract infection (UTI), vitamin deficiencies, or HIV infections.
- Substance-induced conditions such as medication poisoning or carbon monoxide poisoning.

✍ **Note:** Depression can be misdiagnosed as dementia because many of the symptoms appear to be the same. If depression is diagnosed and treated, the dementia-like symptoms can improve.

Since neurocognitive impairment is so commonly found these days, we'll discuss these specific diagnoses in more detail: Alzheimer's, Lewy Bodies, Parkinson's, Vascular and Transtemporal Dementia.

Alzheimer's Disease

Alzheimer's disease is the most common form of dementia and worldwide may contribute to 60-70% of dementia cases. [2]

What is Alzheimer's disease? To most people, it is a very scary word that signals the loss of independence, dignity, and ultimately, personhood. Here are some key facts about this disease.

- The onset of this form of dementia is gradual and progressive.
- The afflicted parent develops multiple cognitive deficits, such as:
  - Memory loss *(this is always present along with at least one or more of the following symptoms)*.
  - Language disturbance.
  - Impaired motor functioning.
  - Inability to recognize or identify objects.
  - Disturbance in the executive functions: planning, organizing, sequencing, and abstract thinking.

These multiple cognitive and physical losses significantly interfere with the person's social or occupational functioning. How and why this happens is still not very clear to the medical profession and, currently, there is no known cure for this disease.

Today, the trend for treatment is toward a more person-centered, individualized, and holistic model.

The key point in assisting an aging parent who is suffering from Alzheimer's disease, or any other type of neurocognitive disorder, is to create an environment that provides:

Safety	Prevent injury, prevent dangerous actions (wandering away).
Structure	Provide a physical and social environment that fosters familiarity and reduces disorientation and anxiety.

---

[2] World Health Organization, "Dementia," (September 21, 2020). https://www.who.int/news-room/fact-sheets/detail/dementia.

Involvement	Create activities as a vehicle for the afflicted person to interact with other people, to laugh, to stay engaged in the human community. The best way to engage a person is through kind, compassionate human contact.
Validation	Respond to the person's cues. Use what you know about your parent to interpret their actions, remarks, or feelings; give them choices whenever possible.

ACTION:
- Be sure to discuss with your parent's physician if you suspect that your aging parent may be showing signs and symptoms of Alzheimer's Disease.
- Request a referral to a neurologist for a more complete assessment.

Lewy Body Dementia

Lewy body dementia is now the second most common neurocognitive disease after Alzheimer's. Lewy body dementia (LBD) is caused by the decay of brain tissues. This decay is caused by the buildup of abnormal proteins called Lewy bodies, which are also found in people with both Alzheimer's disease and Parkinson's disease. Although the earliest signs differ, people with dementia with Lewy bodies or Parkinson's disease dementia may develop similar symptoms over time.

Age is considered the greatest risk factor for LBD as most people who develop this disorder are over age 50. No specific lifestyle factor has been proven to increase one's risk for LBD.

Signs and symptoms of LBD include:
1. Fluctuating cognition with pronounced variations in attention and alertness.
2. Recurrent visual hallucinations that are typically well-formed and detailed.

3. REM sleep behavior disorder (RBD), which may precede cognitive decline.
4. One or more spontaneous features of parkinsonism: speed or slowness of movement, tremors, or rigidity.

✍ **NOTE:** The first three symptoms typically occur early and may persist throughout the course of this disease.

ACTION:
- When your parent's physician considers LBD as a diagnosis, they should check for medication side effects that may mimic LBD symptoms.
- A referral to a neurologist is recommended if the signs and symptoms appear to fall into any one of these categories:
- Progressive cognitive decline, great enough to interfere with normal social or occupational functions or with usual daily activities.
- Prominent or persistent memory impairment *(this may not necessarily occur in the early stages but is usually evident with progression)*.
- Deficits on tests of attention, executive functions and visuo-perceptual ability *(may be especially prominent and occur early)*.

Parkinson's Disease Dementia: (A Major Neurocognitive Disorder)

Parkinson's disease is a brain disorder that leads to shaking, stiffness, and difficulty with walking, balance, and coordination. Parkinson's symptoms usually begin gradually, typically around age 60, and get worse over time. As the disease progresses, people may have difficulty walking and talking. They may also have mental and behavioral changes, sleep problems, depression, memory difficulties, and fatigue. Both men and women can have Parkinson's disease.

Parkinson's Disease Symptoms:
- Tremor (trembling) in hands, arms, legs, jaw, or head
- Stiffness of the limbs and trunk
- Slowness of movement
- Impaired balance and coordination, sometimes leading to falls
- Depression and other emotional changes
- Difficulty swallowing, chewing, and speaking
- Urinary problems or constipation
- Skin problems and sleep disruptions

Parkinson's disease dementia is a form of dementia common in those who have been living with Parkinson's disease for at least a year. It typically appears as a decline in thinking and reasoning due to the brain changes that result from the progression of Parkinson's disease.

As the brain changes caused by Parkinson's gradually spread, they often begin to affect cognitive functions, resulting in:
- Memory loss
- Loss of ability to pay attention
- Poor judgment
- Inability to plan the steps needed to complete a task
- Visual hallucinations, for some

It's estimated that of those diagnosed with Parkinson's, 50 to 80% may experience dementia.[3]

Certain medical tests and responses to drug treatment may help to distinguish them from Parkinson's. Since many other diseases have similar features but require different treatments, **it is important to get an accurate diagnosis as soon as possible**.

---

[3] Alzheimer's Association, "Parkinson's disease dementia." https://www.alz.org/alzheimers-dementia/what-is-dementia/types-of-dementia/parkinson-s-disease-dementia.

ACTION:

- A referral to a neurologist is recommended if the signs and symptoms appear to fall into any one of these categories:
  - Progressive cognitive decline, great enough to interfere with normal social or occupational functions or with usual daily activities.
  - Prominent or persistent memory impairment *(this may not necessarily occur in the early stages but is usually evident with progression).*
  - Deficits on tests of attention, executive functions and visuo-perceptual ability *(may be especially prominent and occur early).*

Vascular Dementia: (A Major Neurocognitive Disorder)

Vascular Dementia is another form of dementia that is common. Vascular Dementia can be caused by a series of small strokes, so it generally has a more abrupt onset and fluctuates with temporary partial remissions and an exacerbation of symptoms.

The cognitive deficits are similar to Alzheimer's disease and may include:

- Memory loss *(generally this is short-term memory loss with any of the following cognitive disturbances)*
- Language problems
- Impaired ability to carry out motor activity: gait and equilibrium disturbances or weakness in extremities *(arms, hands, legs)*
- Failure to recognize familiar objects
- Disturbances in cognitive executive functioning *(planning, organizing, sequencing, abstract thinking)*

It is important to note that vascular dementia can coexist with other forms of dementia, particularly Alzheimer's disease and Lewy body dementia.

```
ACTION:
    • Review and fill out the questionnaires on Signs and Symptoms of
      neurocognitive impairments.
    • Be sure to share this information with your aging parent's
      primary care physician.
    • Your parent's primary care physician can refer your parent
      to specialists in the area of Geriatric Medicine (i.e. neurologist,
      neuropsychologist, vascular or cardiologist) care for a more
      definitive diagnosis and treatment care plan.
    • Another professional service available to assist you is a Geriatric
      Care Manager. They can guide you to the appropriate community
      resources to help you determine what you can do to care for
      your aging parent.
```

Frontotemporal Dementia: (A Major Neurocognitive Disorder)

Formerly called Pick's disease, and sometimes referred to as
frontotemporal disorders, frontotemporal degenerations, and frontal lobe
disorders, this form of dementia refers to a group of disorders caused by
progressive nerve loss in the brain's frontal or temporal lobes.

Symptoms of this form of dementia include:
    • Memory loss
    • Deterioration in behavior
    • Changes in personality
    • Difficulty producing or understanding language

While this form of dementia includes a significant amount of variability
in the symptoms it produces, there are several distinct symptoms, such as
significant changes in behavior, personality traits, or the ability to speak or
understand language.

> **ACTION:**
> - If you see any of these signs of impairment that demonstrate these symptoms, be sure to discuss these with your parent's physician and request an assessment.
> - It is recommended that an assessment be done by a neurologist.

Delirium: (A Major Neurocognitive Disorder)

Delirium is a serious disturbance in mental abilities that results in confused thinking and reduced awareness of the environment. It refers to a new change in mental function that goes well beyond the typical forgetfulness of aging.

Delirium can be thought of as acute brain failure.
- Delirium is usually rapid - symptoms usually can begin over a few hours or a few days.
- The symptoms often fluctuate throughout the day, and there may be periods of no symptoms.
- Symptoms tend to be worse during the night when it's dark and things look less familiar.
- Delirium can often be traced to one or more contributing factors, such as a severe or chronic illness, changes in metabolic balance (such as low sodium), medication, infection, surgery, or alcohol or drug intoxication or withdrawal.

Many of the characteristics of delirium are the same as those of dementia, but delirium develops far more suddenly and can be reversible when its causes are identified and treated.

People with dementia are at high risk of developing delirium, and the two conditions often exist together. Whenever the behavior or thinking of a person with dementia suddenly gets much worse, particularly if the person is sick or in hospital, the cause is likely to be delirium.

Experts have identified three types of delirium:

- **Hyperactive delirium:** Probably the most easily recognized type, this may include restlessness (*for example, pacing*), agitation, rapid mood changes or hallucinations, and refusal to cooperate with care.
- **Hypoactive delirium:** This may include inactivity or reduced motor activity, sluggishness, abnormal drowsiness, or seeming to be in a daze.
- **Mixed delirium:** This includes both hyperactive and hypoactive signs and symptoms. The person may quickly switch back and forth from hyperactive to hypoactive states.

Three of the key signs that a person is delirious are:

1) Difficulty concentrating
2) Changes in behavior, personality, or temperament
3) Change in level of consciousness

Delirium can occur due to many variables:

- Urinary retention or fecal impaction
- History of alcohol or substance abuse
- Infections or sepsis (*respiratory, urinary, or skin*) – Delirium is a strong indicator that a person is seriously ill, and symptoms may be present even before the infection has been discovered.
- Medications – Some medicines commonly used in older adults (*such as heart medicines like digitalis*) can cause delirium in susceptible people.
- Dehydration
- Hospitalization or environmental change – If your parent is hospitalized or experiences an environmental change be sure they have eyeglasses and hearing aids if these are normally used, a clock or watch in easy view, the name of their healthcare providers written clearly in sight, plenty of light during the day (*preferably a window with natural light*), quiet and subdued light or darkness at night, and a family member or friend present whenever possible.

Delirium is considered a medical emergency.

https://www.mayoclinic.org/diseases-conditions/delirium/symptoms-causes/syc-20371386

ACTION:
- If you are aware that your aging parent has not been diagnosed with some type of dementia prior to hospitalization, be sure to get clarification that **this may be delirium**.
- If you suspect that someone in your care with a memory problem has become delirious, you must alert a healthcare professional.

Depression: (A Mental Disorder That is a Risk Factor for Dementia)

Depression can be confused with dementia because many of the symptoms of each are similar.

One ongoing problem of mental health disorders is the fact that your aging parent may be more likely to report physical symptoms rather than mental symptoms, whether they're talking to you or their physician. If you suspect your parent is mentally declining, ask yourself and your parent's physician "Is my parent depressed?"

Depression is one of the most common mental disorders in the elderly, although its exact incidence is difficult to determine. It is frequently unrecognized and therefore untreated. Once depression is recognized and not assumed to be a normal reaction to the many losses and stresses in old age, it is eminently treatable.

Let's identify what depression is and how these symptoms can mimic dementia.
- The elderly may assume that they just don't feel like being active, rather than that they have a depressed mood.
- They also do not often feel comfortable raising concerns about their mental state or how they're feeling emotionally to their physicians since they believe the purpose of the office visit is to discuss physical symptoms.

Here are some characteristic symptoms of depression in the elderly:

Cognitive	Confusion, indecisiveness, poor decision, impaired thinking, difficulty concentrating, impaired memory.
Emotional	Hopelessness, helplessness, worthlessness, tearful, fearful, anxious, worried, irritable, angry, apathetic, bored, depersonalized, sad, feels blue. Suicidal thoughts - plans or behavior.

Changed view of self: Believes self is a failure, inadequate, harmful to others, deserving of punishment, guilty, going crazy. |
| Social | Feels distant from others, has minimal social participation, tends to isolate, lacks interest in activities once enjoyed, withdraws, becomes dependent. |
| Physical | Fatigued, weak, sleep deprived, suffers from insomnia, restless sleep, awakens early, loss of appetite, weight loss, agitation, dizzy spells, psychomotor retardation of speech, gait, etc., headaches, loss of libido, suicidal. |

ACTION:

- You will be a major support to your parent's well-being if you can assist him or her in obtaining the right medical treatment when you observe any of the signs and symptoms of depression.
  - Be sure to notify your parent's physician as soon as you suspect this problem.
  - If your aging parent has been diagnosed with depression, help them seek professional counseling. Seeing a clinical psychologist with a specialty in geriatrics, or a licensed social worker trained in gerontology are preferred professionals to help your aging parent through this problem.

Emotional, Social, Psychological, and Spiritual Needs.

Your aging parent has unique emotional, social, psychological, and spiritual needs that evolve as the aging process occurs. As your parent(s) age, they may feel useless, lonely, angry, or even in denial about their wellness and capabilities. Living alone may further exacerbate negative feelings.

All these needs should be taken into consideration for the best possible care. First, we need to explore the emotional needs of the elderly.

Sign and Symptoms: Your Parent's Emotional Needs

Why are Emotions important to understand? Emotions help us:

- To act, survive, strike, or avoid danger.
- To make decisions.
- To understand others. Moreover, they help other people understand us.

As your parent ages, they have many emotions in response to the changes they are going through. Their functional abilities are changing, and perhaps they are beginning to have some health concerns and cognitive issues. These changes weigh heavily on the aging adult.

Emotions help identify when something needs to change *(thoughts or attitudes or something in our relationships or environment)*. There is a lot of wisdom in all our emotions, including those we think are negative.

- If you're feeling sad, there's probably something you need to let go of, such as a loss, dream, or goal.
- If you're feeling anxious, there's probably something you need to face or address. This could be something from your past, something in your present, or something you're worrying will happen in the future.
- If you're feeling angry, there's probably something you feel isn't fair, and you need to identify what it is.

In each case, if you deny or shove away the emotion, you won't be able to tap into the information it has for you. Ignoring your emotions and needs can begin to show up in our relationships with others. We may unintentionally come off as abrupt, annoyed, or disinterested. This, in turn, can negatively impact our relationships.

There are 3 critical emotional needs to watch for when considering the well-being and emotional health of your aging parent, and when to get more involved.

1) **Safety & Security:** Most elderly adults' greatest fear is falling. A safe, secure environment for older adults is crucial to their well-being.
   - Is their environment safe and free from obstacles and clutter.
   - Can they manage to get to their kitchen, bathroom, and bedroom safely?
   - Are they locking their doors?
   - Do they have a security system in place, such as an alarm, or emergency response system?

2) **Connection**: The feeling of being disconnected emotionally and physically from people can be detrimental to your parent's health.
   - Isolation is a very real problem when your aging parent cannot get out of their home unless someone helps them.
   - Loss of friends and no stimulating conversation or activity can quickly reduce your aging parent's sense of well-being and cause mental decline.

3) **Autonomy:** Relying on others can be a tough transition for them.
   - Your parent has been independent most of their adult life.
   - It becomes very difficult to adjust to reliance on others to meet their daily needs.

Sign and Symptoms: What are the Social Needs of Elderly Adults?

There are two social needs of the elderly that can counteract and even prevent isolation and loneliness.

1) Meaningful Relationships
   - Older adults require meaningful relationships and experiences.
   - They want to know that you genuinely care about them.
   - Be sure to call your aging family members regularly to check in.

Here are a few ideas to get the conversation going:
   - Ask them for a recap of their day.
   - Ask them how they're feeling (mentally, emotionally, etc).
   - Ask them if they've invested time into a new or existing hobby.
   - Ask about their childhood and what life was like back then to work out their memory muscles.
   - Ask open-ended questions to prompt a long response. They want to know that their thoughts and input are valuable to you.
   - Be present. The best thing you can do in a conversation with an older adult is listen.

2) Social Interactions
   - Social interactions can play a positive role in counteracting cognitive decline.
   - Encourage visits with peers, friends, and relatives whenever possible.
   - Encourage your aging parent or arrange for them to visit senior centers, church services, etc.

Sign and Symptoms: What are the Psychological Needs of Elderly Adults?

More than 2 million Americans aged 65 and older live with some form of depression. As a family member of an older adult, you can provide mental stimulation when you can. Here are some suggestions:

- Play memory games.
- Offer a space for them to express their genuine thoughts and feelings.
- Give elderly parents a scrapbook and ask if they can recall positive memories.
- Ask your aging parent to repeat something they just said or reminisce about past experiences to help their cognitive functions, even if it's over the phone.

Sign and Symptoms: Spirituality-What You Need to Know?

Why is spirituality important? First, let's look at the different ways spirituality has been defined over the last few decades.

In response to the 1971 White House Conference on Aging, the National Interfaith Coalition on Aging (organized in 1972) defined spirituality as *"the affirmation of life in relationship with God, self, community, and the environment that nurtures and celebrates wholeness."*[4]

Christina Puchalski, MD, director of the George Washington Institute for Spirituality and Health, contends that *"spirituality is the part of all human beings that searches for meaning, purpose, and connection to others."*[5] It is the way they experience their connectedness to the moment, self, others, nature, and the significant or sacred.

Basically, spirituality is defined as a belief system focusing on intangible elements that provide meaning to life's events.

---

[4] 1971 White House Conference on Aging, A Report to the Delegates from the Conference Sections and Special Concerns Sessions, Nov 28-Dec 2, Section: Spiritual Well Being, page 24.

[5] GWish founder and Executive Director, Christina Puchalski, MD, FACP, FAAHPM https://smhs.gwu.edu/spirituality-health/about-gwish#MessagePuchalski.

Understanding Your Parent's Spirituality

In the first half of life, each of us (including your aging parent) is focused on survival and quantity of life experiences. We make new contacts and establish relationships. We focus on our careers or raising our family and developing a financial base for our security.

Currently, your aging parent's focus on life is different from yours.

- Your parent is more interested in exerting less energy, or more aptly put, they need to get a deeper return for the energy he or she expends.
- Your parent may be more contemplative and selective about how they spend time.
- Your parent may begin to spend time in ways he or she never did before (gardening, taking walks, listening to music, or just talking about life, feelings, or dreams once held).

As your parent ages, this reflection on life becomes very important for you to understand. What you are noticing is one of the major life tasks each of us arrives at as we age:

Redefining our purpose and meaning in life.

One way to increase your understanding of your parent's view of life is to explore his or her spirituality.

Emotional Health and Spirituality-How Are These Related?

While motions and spirituality are distinct, they are also linked and integrated with one another. Your parent's emotional health and spirituality go hand-in-hand as the well-being in each arena influences and overlaps with the other:

- Spirituality is about seeking a meaningful connection with something bigger than yourself, which can result in positive emotions such as peace, awe, contentment, gratitude, and acceptance.
- Emotional health is about cultivating a positive state of mind, which can broaden your outlook to recognize and incorporate a sense of calm or well-being.

When both emotional and spiritual needs are met, a general sense of well-being that fosters a connection to other people and the world as a whole is created.

As your parent ages, they may begin to feel more isolated and alone – which can promote the negative aspects of aging and lead to depression, fatigue, and further isolation. Paying attention to both emotional and spiritual needs may counteract this by offering more peace, contentment, and acceptance of the changes in their life.

What if Your Parent has Dementia?

Meeting spiritual needs when your parent has dementia is incredibly important. In fact, this may be the hook that brings them back to a level of awareness and communication with the people who are most meaningful to them.

Dementia may seem to mask the need for spirituality, but the reality is that, from my experience, cognitive impairment does not eclipse our innate need as human beings for inner peace, comfort, prayer, and rituals.

Spirituality calls back experiences that may have occurred early on in your parent's life, which in turn can help them remember what means the most to them. Helping your parent emotionally connect with their spiritual beliefs is important to their overall well-being. No matter what your parent's current situation is (including dementia), if you can replicate and maintain as much of this arena of their life as possible it will be very helpful to their peace of mind and well-being.

Benefits of Spirituality

One of the main benefits of spirituality is the strong sense of community at the heart of most faith groups. People form and strengthen relationships through their faith, whether it's by attending group services or just praying with a friend. These opportunities for social interactions are especially important to seniors, who are at risk of becoming isolated as they age. These social bonds can be particularly comforting during difficult times.

Many seniors must also cope with the loss of a spouse or loved one. Others might be grappling with their own illness or mortality. Faith can provide a support system for handling these tough issues. For some, end-of-life issues might bring up unpleasant past experiences that may need to be reconciled in some way, and having a supportive spiritual environment can help minimize distress and move one toward acceptance and resolution.

So, this leaves the question of how does religion relate to spirituality? While it is not necessary to be "religious" to have spirituality, it is important to understand the relationship between religion and spirituality. Religion and spirituality are not the same thing, nor are they entirely distinct from one another. The two can overlap in several ways.

- In spirituality, the questions posed are: where do I personally find meaning, connection, and value?
- In religion, the questions are: what is true and right?
- An individual's experiences significantly shape their thoughts, feelings, and behaviors, affecting their spiritual journey.
- Religion is the formal structure of shared beliefs and practices that sets it apart from spirituality.
- It is important to understand that it is possible to develop spirituality outside of the structure of traditional religious organizations. All aspects of our lives, such as music, nature, art, architecture, etc., can help us develop spirituality.

As a caregiver, it is spirituality as a dimension of human nature, rather than religion, that is important to consider. If your parent is practicing a specific religion or has in the past, this is a very important area to explore. On the other hand, if they have not or will not consider religion, do not force the issue. Spirituality can be developed and explored in many productive and enhancing ways, without the requirement that your parent be part of an organized religion.

How to Support Spirituality

When someone is nearing the end of their life, taking care of their spiritual needs becomes very important. It can reduce stress and worry and help them feel calmer. Exploring what has provided meaning throughout their life, as well as identifying the beliefs or sources of strength that will sustain them as they approach the end, can bring great comfort to their final days.

The keys to supporting spirituality is to connect with your aging parent and know what's important to them. Spiritual needs are different for everyone, so it's vital to learn how you can best spiritually support your parent as an individual. Here are a few ideas:

- Seeking opportunities to connect through everyday encounters like sharing stories and memories.
- Respecting their personal identity, culture, and diversity, and allowing them freedom to express themselves and their beliefs.
- Providing appropriate and understandable information in supporting choice and decision-making.
- Facilitating overall wellness by encouraging engagement in purposeful activities (*such as providing raised garden beds for those interested in gardening, or arranging music and well-being programs*).
- Providing the opportunity to access quiet outdoor areas and natural spaces.
- Facilitating prayer or meditation and providing access to religious services.

- Encouraging them to reflect on their memories and experiences.
- Providing support for important relationships with families.
- Being present and compassionate.

There are a lot of activities that touch the soul and enhance spirituality. Some suggestions are in Chapter 10 - *Taking Care of You*. These activities can also be used with your aging parent. These activities can provide peace and support as they are going through their lifestyle changes.

ACTION:
- Try to keep your parent in touch with what has had meaning and sustaining value to him or her in the past.
- If your parent has never been a part of an organized religion or can no longer relate to a religion that he or she once accepted, do not feel you must connect him or her with religion to enhance spirituality.

2

Assessment Tools

IN THIS CHAPTER:

- **Real Stories About the Assessment Process**
- **Functional Assessment**
- **Questionnaire: Identifying Your Parent's Daily Living**
- **Questionnaire: Assessing Your Parent's Daily Activities**
- **Questionnaire: Identifying Your Parent's Ability to Handle More Complex Tasks of Independent Living**
- **Cognitive Assessment**
- **Questionnaire: Mental & Neurocognitive Symptoms**
- **Emotional Assessment**
- **Questionnaire: Identifying Emotional Symptoms**
- **Questionnaire: Identifying Symptoms of Depression**
- **Geriatric Depression Scale**
- **Spirituality Assessment**
- **Defining Spirituality**
- **Spirituality & Emotional Health**
- **Questionnaire: Identifying Your Parent's Spiritual Needs**
- **Questionnaire: Identifying Spiritual Pain**
- **Behavioral Assessment**
- **Questionnaire: Social & Behavioral Assessment**
- **Questionnaire: Identifying Online Behavior Symptoms**
- **Living Arrangements for Your Aging Parent**
- **Identifying the Right Level of Care for Your Parent**
- **Instructions for Using Living Arrangements Assessment**

Real Stories About the Assessment Process

The initial questionnaire is just for making observations, not diagnoses. The goal is to notice any patterns in your parent's behaviors or responses. These observed patterns can then be given to professionals, who will use them to help make an official clinical assessment and diagnosis.

The person most involved in an aging parent's care typically ends up being the main recipient of the doctor's diagnoses, treatment plans, and recommendations. Just like you initially observed patterns in your parent's behavior and reported them to the primary care physician, your role now is to understand the information given back to you. This information includes the diagnosis, treatment, prescribed medicines, and level of assistance or safety measures required for your parent. With the knowledge you have gained, your job shifts to figuring out how to properly take care of and manage your parent's needs according to the doctor's orders.

The key takeaway here is that the initial questionnaire is just for making observations, not diagnoses – leave them to the doctors.

Story of JoAnne

JoAnne collapsed at home and was fortunately found by her neighbors. She was taken to the hospital and treated for a UTI but was also diagnosed with dementia during her stay. Upon discharge, the neighbors called JoAnne's sister and said, "She is highly confused and needs someone to watch over her." The sister called me and said, "She reads, she doesn't appear to be demented in any way, but what she does appear is to be profoundly sad. She's just crying a lot."

I said, "Okay, that's probably part of why she collapsed. She's not eating and drinking." The sister stated, "But now every time she goes to the doctor or we want to have her treated, they basically look at the records and say she has dementia."

So, this took advocacy on our part. I called her primary care physician, with the permission of the sister, and got her evaluated by a clinical psychologist. The psychologist said, "If she wasn't depressed, she certainly is now having to fight this battle that she's not demented."

But yes, JoAnne was depressed, and they identified what the cause of that depression was and started to treat her.

In her case, I had a resource that corrected things to a certain point, but there was still more work to do because she had records now, medical records that stated she had dementia. However, she didn't, she was depressed, which is a mental health problem. I took her in to see her primary care physician, and said, "What are we going to do about this? Because on her medical record in the hospital, they misdiagnosed her." And he said, "All right, I'm going to call the doctor that diagnosed her. I'm going to ask him to amend his diagnosis, and I will write an addendum to the medical record." So, we got this done for JoAnne and her family, but it took time and effort to do so.

Story of Louise

When we were first asked to come in by Louise's out-of-town family, she had the diagnoses of Parkinson's. In addition to that, she was starting to have more difficulty taking care of herself. This was because the disorder affected her ability to handle basic personal care tasks. She needed somebody standing by because she could easily fall, and she needed help with shopping because she really shouldn't drive. But she could articulate what she wanted to eat, what she wanted someone to buy for her, how frequently she wanted to take her shower, and what medications she was taking.

Pretty soon I started to notice that not only was Louise struggling, but she'd start to get confused and ask, "Where are we going? Why are we going there?" when I would come to get her.

It was clear the Parkinson's had advanced to a level of cognitive impairment that needed to be addressed. So, we completed our assessment questions and brought them to her physicians. We then had a specialist who looked at the Parkinson's for us and a behavioral neurologist who took care of the diagnosis.

They pretty much decided that Louise had dementia brought on by the Parkinson's (the brain starts to deteriorate when you have Parkinson's). So that's what was going on with her but then she had some other issues that were impacting her heart and vision too.

The point being made here is that when you are working with and caring for your parent, make sure you are bringing any new symptoms to the attention of the medical power of attorney and/or the physician. Diseases can parallel each other and impact the body in many ways. You must know how to distinguish these issues so your parent is properly medicated. This is where your observations come in. You don't have to do the diagnosing as the caregiver, you just have to update the physicians on what it is you are seeing and recognizing, and what feedback the family is giving. Because then they can gather all this new information and come up with the correct diagnosis. This wasn't about Parkinson's. Yes, Louise had a primary diagnosis of Parkinson's, but it looked to us like she had a cardiac issue as well.

In summary, when someone completes the assessment, they note their observations. These assessments are taken to the parent's primary care physician, who will determine if further evaluation is needed. If so, they will follow up with a referral to the appropriate specialists.

As a Geriatric Care Manager, we can provide the client's healthcare team with a detailed rationale to investigate further what may be underlying the client's current condition or situation. That's our job to make sure our client is getting the best care possible from all those on their healthcare team.

The following information and questionnaires are included only to assist you in organizing your observations so you can communicate more effectively and efficiently with your parent's physician. They are not intended to define or diagnose the problem.

Functional Assessment: How Well is Your Parent Managing Independent Living?

The focus of this section is determining how well your parent is currently functioning at home. Illness does not necessarily create barriers to safe independent living. Likewise, your parent's poor mental status does not always mean they cannot remain independent. Knowing how your parent is functioning at home can guide you in knowing what type of services might be needed to keep him or her safe.

To get an adequate overview of how your parent is functioning at home, you must observe them yourself or rely upon an unbiased friend or family member to assist you. If possible, the best resource to gather this information would be a professional, such as a neuropsychologist, geriatric care manager, physical therapist, or occupational therapist who is trained in conducting this type of assessment in the home.

Questionnaire #1: Identifying Your Parent's Ability to Handle Activities of Daily Living

This rating system is designed to assess and distinguish your parent's ability to perform daily living activities.

1) Independent (parent needs no assistance)
2) Assistance (parent needs part-time assistance)
3) Dependent (parent cannot perform task without assistance)

Check the most accurate description of your parent's current level of function for that activity:

Bathing (sponge, shower, or tub)

☐ Needs no assistance (can get in/out of tub/shower without help).
☐ Needs some assistance in bathing (only one part of the body).
☐ Needs assistance in bathing (cannot manage safely).

Dressing

☐ Can get clothes and put them on without assistance.
☐ Can get clothes and put them on but cannot manage to clothe either the upper body or lower body without help.
☐ Cannot get dressed without assistance (or stays undressed).

Toileting

- ☐ Goes to the bathroom, maintains personal hygiene, and arranges clothes without assistance (may utilize assistive devices, such as cane, walker, wheelchair, for support, and may manage using and cleaning a night bedpan).
- ☐ Must have assistance in going to the bathroom, cleaning self, or arranging clothes after elimination or in the use of night bedpan or commode.
- ☐ Does not go to the bathroom for the elimination process.

Transfer

- ☐ Can move in/out of bed, in/out of a chair without assistance (may use an assistive device, such as cane or walker for support).
- ☐ Can move in/out of bed or chair with assistance.
- ☐ Cannot get out of bed or chair.

Continence

- ☐ Can control urination and bowel movement completely.
- ☐ Has occasional accidents.
- ☐ Needs supervision to maintain urine and bowel control.

Feeding

- ☐ Feeds self without assistance (uses utensils).
- ☐ Feeds self except for cutting food.
- ☐ Needs assistance in feeding or is fed partly or completely.

(Adapted from the Katz Index of ADL)[1]

ACTION:

- If your parent cannot perform the tasks of daily living, you will need to assess what level of in-home support and assistance is required to adequately address their needs.
- If you cannot provide this care for your parent at home, where is the least restrictive environment this can be offered?

---

[1] Alzheimer's Association, "Katz Index of Independence in Activities of Daily Living." https://www.alz.org/careplanning/downloads/katz-adl.pdf.

Questionnaire #2: Identifying Your Parent's Ability to Handle More Complex Tasks of Independent Living

This rating system is designed to assess and distinguish your parent's ability to perform daily living activities.

1) Independent (parent needs no assistance)
2) Assistance (parent needs part-time assistance)
3) Dependent (parent cannot perform task without assistance)

Check the most accurate description of your parent's current level of function for that activity:

Telephone/Cell Phone

☐ Able to look up numbers, dial, receive, and make calls without help.

☐ Able to answer the phone or dial an operator in an emergency, but still needs help with typical telephone use.

☐ Unable to use the telephone.

Special Consideration: Technology

There are many ways to reach out and connect with the world Your parent may do this through the use of their phone or they may use the various avenues on their computer (social media platforms, video calls, etc.). The point is to understand how they're connecting to their world without focusing on how well they use a given technology.

Transportation (Travel)

☐ Able to drive, travel alone, or use a bus or taxi without help.

☐ Able to travel but needs assistance and cannot go alone.

☐ Unable to drive or manage transportation alone.

Shopping

☐ Able to take care of all shopping needs (may need transportation and this may include online shopping).

☐ Able to do shopping but not alone.

☐ Unable to do any shopping.

Meal Preparation

- ☐ Able to plan and cook full meals.
- ☐ Able to prepare light foods and operate a microwave but not able to prepare and cook full meals.
- ☐ Unable to prepare meals.

This section is focused on their ability to plan and cook their meals—it is not addressing their ability to call out and order food (either directly to the restaurant or through a food delivery app) because that's a different skill. Knowing where your parent is in this skill makes it much easier for the family to help because you can have meals sent in to ensure proper nutrition and support if needed.

Housework

- ☐ Able to do all housework and laundry chores.
- ☐ Able to do only light housework but needs help with heavy tasks.
- ☐ Unable to do any housework or laundry.

It's important for your parent's home to be livable, not only for their physical health but also for their mental well-being and overall quality of life.

Money Management

- ☐ Able to manage buying needs, writing checks, and paying bills.
- ☐ Able to manage daily buying needs but needs help with the checkbook and paying bills.
- ☐ Unable to manage money.

Does your parent understand how much money they have? This is a very sensitive area because they may feel you are asking them to give up control to a key area of their life. This is also a place where they can be very vulnerable to predators.

Be sure to see Chapter 9 - Abuse Predators, opportunists, for more indepth information.

Medication Management
- ☐ Able to take medication in the right doses and at the right times.
- ☐ Able to take medication but needs reminding or someone to prepare it.
- ☐ Unable to take medication and needs someone to administer it.

(Adapted from the Katz Index of ADL)[2]

ACTION:
- If your parent cannot perform the tasks listed above, you will need to determine how to provide assistance in the home to meet these needs. Any time you have an answer that falls into a 2 or 3, you know it's time to get help.
- Often there are community resources in your parent's city, county, and state that can help you meet your parent's needs.
- It is also important to understand that while these assessments are simple, they're just the beginning!
- Once you have an understanding how your parent is functioning in each of these areas, you need to determine how best to help them.

Cognitive Assessment: What are the Mental & Neurocognitive Symptoms?

The human mind is a miraculous and complex system. It controls how we think, feel, and move. It governs everything we do from driving a car to anticipating the day to feeling happy or sad to managing relationships with friends and family. Cognitive impairment can significantly change a person's life as well as the lives of the people close to them.

Cognitive functioning refers to how your parent thinks and processes information. Memory, attention, organization, planning, and perception are the intellectual functions that make up your parent's cognitive abilities.

---

[2] Alzheimer's Association, "Katz Index of Independence in Activities of Daily Living." https://www.alz.org/careplanning/downloads/katz-adl.pdf.

Here is a list of cognitive functions that can be affected by problems of the brain:

Attention and Concentration	The ability to focus on one task while being able to block out distractions.
Planning	The ability to look ahead, direct, initiate, and monitor his or her activities.
Memory	The ability to receive, store, and retrieve pieces of information.
Communication Skills	The ability to have speech and understanding of language and to formulate thoughts.
Abstraction and Judgment	Abstraction is the ability to take a specific situation or information and apply or generalize it to another similar situation. Judgment is the ability to understand the consequences of options and determine the appropriateness of the action.
Learning	The ability to acquire new information, retain it, generalize it to similar tasks, and make it a part of his or her knowledge base.
Fund of Knowledge	The commonly known facts and information retained throughout life.

Significant changes in these areas of functioning will interfere with your parent's daily living routines.

Do you think your parent has shown changes in one or more of the mental abilities listed previously?

☐ Yes ☐ No ☐ Don't know

Write down any new behaviors you have observed. Use as your guideline from the symptoms listed previously.

_____

_____

_____

_____

Use this questionnaire to identify any cognitive limitations or symptoms.

Questionnaire #3: Identifying Mental & Neurocognitive Symptoms

☑ Check each statement that best describes your parent's current behavior.

It's important to rule out any medical issues before considering any cognitive symptoms. For example, if your parent simply cannot hear well, but is too embarrassed to acknowledge this limitation or ask you to speak slowly or loudly, then it will be hard for them to answer many of these questions.

☐ Your parent has a problem remembering appointments due to memory loss.

☐ Your parent forgets to take medication prescribed by a physician.

☐ Your parent does not know what day it is.

☐ Your parent does not know what month it is.

☐ Your parent does not know what year it is.

☐ Your parent cannot tell you where he or she lives: city, state, county.

☐ Your parent cannot subtract 3 from 20, then keep subtracting from each new number, all the way to zero.

☐ Your parent is unable to recognize you or other familiar people all the time.

☐ Your parent has difficulty remembering words.

☐ Your parent cannot understand what is said to her or him.

☐ Your parent has difficulty learning new tasks or information.

☐ Your parent has difficulty with problem-solving.

☐ Your parent makes poor decisions but seems unaware of the consequences.

☐ Your parent is confused.

☐ Your parent cannot interpret the meaning of a proverb, i.e., "the early bird catches the worm."

> **ACTION:**
> - Identify signs or symptoms of cognitive limitations.
> - Request that a Mental Status Examination be administered by their primary care physician, neurologist, neuropsychologist, psychologist, or licensed social worker.

I also recommend requesting a Montreal Cognitive Assessment (MoCA) to be conducted by a trained professional if you observe subtle changes in your parent's neurocognitive functioning. The Montreal Cognitive Assessment is validated as a highly sensitive tool for early detection of mild cognitive impairment [3]

MoCA accurately and quickly assesses: [4]

- Short term memory
- Visuospatial abilities
- Executive functions
- Attention, concentration, and working memory
- Language
- Orientation to time and place

Emotional Assessment: What are the Emotional Symptoms?

When your aging parent begins to lose some cognitive functioning, they may begin to express anger, frustration, sadness, hostility, and depression.

Listed below are some common personality changes that can occur.

☑ **Check** any symptoms you have observed:

- ☐ Mood swings
- ☐ Emotional outbursts, unreasonable rage, or anger
- ☐ Lack of emotional response (flatness in affect, looks vague or vacant)
- ☐ Anxiety
- ☐ Irritability

---

[3] https://www.mocatest.org/the-moca-test
[4] https://www.mocatest.org/the-moca-test

☐ Hostility
☐ Stubbornness
☐ Loss of sense of humor
☐ Suspiciousness
☐ Jealousy
☐ Fearfulness

Have you noticed any changes in your parent's usual way of coping with everyday life events?

☐ Yes   ☐ No   ☐ Don't know

Write down any new behaviors you have observed. Use as your guideline from the symptoms listed previously.

_____

_____

_____

_____

_____

Use this questionnaire to identify emotional symptoms of impairment.

Questionnaire #4: Identifying Emotional Symptoms

☑ **Check each statement that is true for your parent:**
   ☐ Your parent has emotional outbursts or displays temper tantrums.
   ☐ Your parent looks bored or vacant.
   ☐ Your parent complains of feeling nervous, jittery, or edgy.
   ☐ Your parent is easily annoyed or provoked to anger.
   ☐ Your parent has become increasingly impatient.
   ☐ Your parent is belligerent, aggressive, and/or hostile.
   ☐ Your parent has become very opinionated or obstinate.
   ☐ Your parent no longer has a sense of humor.
   ☐ Your parent has developed a sense of humor during anxious times. *

☐ Your parent is suspicious without cause.

☐ Your parent gets unhappy or confrontational if he/she is not the center of your attention.

While this may not be a behavior to be concerned about in isolation, it can indicate that your parent is putting on a good facade to relieve anxiety associated with the loss of cognitive functioning.

ACTION:
- Communicate your observations with your parent's primary care physician or neurologist. They can help you interpret these observations accurately and may refer your parent to healthcare professionals, such as psychologists, neurologists, or social workers, for guidance on managing emotional symptoms.
- Part of the Emotional signs and symptom that may be creating a barrier to safe and adequate functioning is the possibility your parent may be depressed.
- This symptom can present as a neurocognitive impairment (Dementia) or metabolic problems. It is important to identify what you are observing to get the proper diagnosis and treatment for your parent.

Questionnaire #5: Identifying Symptoms of Depression

This questionnaire is crucial as it assists in identifying depression in your aging parent, a known risk factor for dementia. Early identification and treatment may help in preventing a dementia diagnosis.

☑ **Check statements that are true of your parent's current behavior:**

- ☐ Your parent's sad mood seems out of proportion to circumstances.
- ☐ Your parent shows a loss of interest in life.
- ☐ Your parent has given up friends and social contacts.
- ☐ Your parent has displayed a change in appetite.
- ☐ Your parent has had suicidal thoughts, plans, or attempts.
- ☐ Your parent has a loss of libido.
- ☐ Your parent has had an increase in sleep disturbances (too much, not enough, or fitful).
- ☐ Your parent has exhibited a decrease in cognitive function or physical activity.
- ☐ Your parent has difficulty concentrating or paying attention.
- ☐ Your parent has consistent displays of memory loss, forgetfulness, or word loss.

ACTION:
- Check all statements
- Consult your parent's primary care physician immediately.
- There are specific treatment concerns that only the physician can determine, and it's important to avoid trying to make any kind of diagnosis of the problem on your own.
- Support your parent in communicating frankly with the physician.

Geriatric Depression Scale

This is a short form of the Geriatric Depression Scale. You can use it for your parent as a self-assessment tool or you can read these questions to your parent and record his or her answers.

Score one point for each response that matches the yes or no answer after each question. In other words, if your parent's response is "yes" to a question and the answer in parenthesis is "(yes)", score one point. If your parent's response is "no" to a question, but the answer in the parenthesis is "(yes)", do not score one point.

	Answer Yes or No	Pts.
1. Are you satisfied with your life? (No)		
2. Have you dropped many of your activities and interests? (Yes)		
3. Do you feel that your life is empty? (Yes)		
4. Do you often get bored? (Yes)		
5. Are you in good spirits most of the time? (No)		
6. Are you afraid that something bad is going to happen to you? (Yes)		
7. Do you feel happy most of the time? (Yes)		
8. Do you often feel helpless? (Yes)		
9. Do you prefer to stay in at night, rather than go out and do new things? (Yes)		
10. Do you feel you have more problems with memory than most people? (Yes)		
11. Do you think it is wonderful to be alive now? (No)		
12. Do you feel pretty worthless the way you are now? (Yes)		
13. Do you feel full of energy? (No)		
14. Do you think that most persons are better off than you are? (Yes)		
15. Do you have trouble concentrating? (Yes)		
Total:		

(Sheikh & Savage, 1986)

✎ **NOTE:**

A score of five points or more may indicate depression. If your parent's score indicates depression, consult with his/her physician for recommendations.

Spirituality Assessment: What You Need to Know About Your Parent's Spirituality

Spirituality is among the many complex issues that you need to address as you assess the needs of your aging parent. This area of your parent's life may not initially be on your list of issues to think about, but you will gain a deeper understanding of "who" your aging parent is at this stage in life by doing so.

Defining Spirituality

For some people, spirituality and faith are deeply intertwined—whether it's a devotion to God, Buddha, or simply a belief in something larger than oneself. Yet for others, spirituality may manifest as a restorative bond with nature, a soothing connection with music, or a profound exploration of self-awareness. Spirituality is a broad concept, but in essence, it is about:

- Seeking a sense of purpose and meaning
- Feeling a sense of belonging and connectedness
- Needing to feel hope and gratitude
- Connecting to something bigger than ourselves

Spirituality is a universal human experience that touches us all. It can be described as sacred, transcendent, or a deep sense of being alive and connected. It begs the questions about life and identity, such as:

- Am I a good person?
- What is the meaning of my suffering?
- What is my connection to the world around me?
- Do things happen for a reason?
- How can I live my life in the best way possible?

The spiritual life of your elderly parent may be intricately linked to their association with a church, temple, mosque, or synagogue. However, it is important to understand that religion and spirituality are not the same things, nor are they entirely distinct from one another.

Spirituality and Emotional Health

Emotions and spirituality, though distinct, can also be intricately linked and seamlessly integrated with each other.

Spirituality is about seeking a meaningful connection with something bigger than yourself, which can result in positive emotions, such as peace, awe, contentment, gratitude, and acceptance.

Emotional health is about cultivating a positive state of mind, which can broaden your outlook to recognize and incorporate a connection to something larger than yourself.

Spiritual care often holds greater importance at the end of one's life. Spiritual care can reduce stress as a person faces death, helping them explore what has given meaning to their lives and what will sustain them as they face their final days.

The key to supporting spirituality is to connect with your aging parent and know what's important to them.

```
┌─────────────────────────────────────────────────────────────────┐
│ ACTION:                                                           │
│ •  Identify the name, address, and phone number of your parent's  │
│    spiritual leaders (minister, priest, rabbi, etc.). With your   │
│    parent's permission, contact this person to request            │
│    observations on how well your parent is managing.              │
│ •  Request any information about community support that is        │
│    available to your parent through this person's organization.   │
│                                                                   │
│ Name              Address                          Phone          │
│ _____  │
│                                                                   │
│ _____  │
│                                                                   │
│ _____  │
│                                                                   │
│ _____  │
└─────────────────────────────────────────────────────────────────┘
```

Questionnaire #6: Identifying Your Parent's Spiritual Needs

Listed below are several human needs that are a part of spirituality. Evaluate each in terms of your parent's current activities.

Does Your Parent:	Still Does	Used to	Never Did
Believe that life is meaningful and has a purpose.			
Feel a sense of unity with others and has meaningful relationships			
Feel appreciated and respected			
Feel he/she is listened to, and that what they believe or say matters to others.			
Feels he/she is growing in faith; is still learning and practicing whatever values that faith professes.			

If any of these needs are not being met, your parent may be experiencing low or poor self-esteem. Parents who have lost their sense of value and worth are usually harder to care for because of their lack of motivation and loss of interest in living.

Questionnaire #7: Identifying Spiritual Pain

The following are some symptoms that could be attributed to spiritual pain. Does your parent show signs of any of them? Be careful not to impose your beliefs on your parent. Also do not jump to the conclusion from this list that your parent needs to attend a formal religious service to relieve his or her pain. These symptoms are merely a reference point to see if your parent is missing the peace that accompanies a spiritual nature.

Check "Yes" or "No" for each symptom as applicable.

Yes	No	
		Nonspecific sorrow or grief
		Isolation from others
		Feels life is meaningless
		Feels life is empty or hollow
		Fears the future and avoids talking about it
		Has a sense of hopelessness and despair
		Is angry and bitter toward God

✍ NOTE:
If your parent exhibits any of these symptoms, contact your parent's spiritual leader to enlist their help in meeting your parent's spiritual needs.

Behavioral Assessment: What are the Social Behavior Symptoms?

Each person is unique as he/she ages, and each person is influenced by life experiences differently. There is no typical "old person" behavior, although many people think there is (This is a form of ageism that is discriminatory and harmful to any elderly person who lives today.) Listed below are changes in social behavior that may be warning signals of mental impairment. While many of the following may not seem to be symptoms, it is important to recognize them as such.

Loss of Initiative	Lack of spontaneity, needs direction for most activities.
Loss of Interest	Withdraws from social relationships, is unresponsive or apathetic.
Restlessness	In contrast to apathetic, acts confused, rummaging through drawers or shuffling papers.
Loosening of Inhibitions	Displays poor social judgment.
Impulsiveness	Makes imprudent decisions.
Verbal Changes	Makes up stories to accommodate for failing memory, constantly talks about the same thing over and over, or talks about nonsense topics as though they are significant topics.
Personal Neglect	A very important clue to serious problems, especially if the person normally performs personal care tasks.
Incontinence	If there is no apparent physical reason, this in an indicator of mental impairment.

Have you noticed any of these changes in your parent's behavior?

☐ Yes ☐ No ☐ Don't know

If yes, which changes appear to be occurring now? Write them down here:

_____

_____

_____

Questionnaire #8: Identifying Social Behavior Signs & Symptoms

☑ Check each statement that currently describes your parent's behavior.

- ☐ Your parent needs direction for most activities.
- ☐ Your parent has stopped being spontaneous.
- ☐ Your parent can start activities but seems unable or unwilling to finish.
- ☐ Your parent has started to withdraw or has withdrawn from social activities.
- ☐ Your parent is no longer taking good or adequate personal care, such as bathing, shaving, wearing clean clothes, etc.
- ☐ Your parent is hyperactive (restless, rummaging or shuffling through papers) or has begun to wander aimlessly.
- ☐ Your parent displays inappropriate social behavior, which is embarrassing to you and to others.
- ☐ Your parent does not appear to recognize the inappropriateness of his or her behavior.
- ☐ Your parent is no longer cautious about managing financial affairs or has made imprudent disclosures or decisions.
- ☐ Your parent talks about events that are not accurate. At one time he or she knew the correct facts but now appears unaware of the inaccuracy.
- ☐ Your parent constantly talks about just one event.
- ☐ Your parent's conversations are nonsense or irrelevant to the content of the discussion yet he or she seems unaware of this problem.

Questionnaire #9: Identifying Online Behavior Signs & Symptoms

☑ Check each statement that currently describes your parent's behavior.

- ☐ Your parent is taking a large amount of money out of the bank or other cash accounts and sending it to a person or group they met online.
- ☐ Your parent spends a lot of time watching the online shopping channels and is making unnecessary purchases. (Many of the shopping channels make offers that may entice your parent to buy items that are not needed.)
- ☐ Your parent has been talking to company salespersons (*as a result of online activity*) about buying items or arranging appointments to make home repairs.
- ☐ Your parent is making new friends online that they don't know in person.

✐ **NOTE:**

Observe for warning signs, so if you have checked one or many of these statements you need to consult with your parent's primary care physician, geriatric care manager, geriatric psychologist, or request a referral to a neurologist.

Living Arrangements for Your Aging Parent: What You Need to Know

There are multiple variables that need to be considered whenever you are determining the appropriate type of living arrangement for your parent.

First, it's incredibly important to understand that unless your parent is deemed incompetent by a judge, his or her consent is always required before any action is taken to change your parent's residence permanently. If they are determined to be incompetent, you need to have both medical power of attorney and financial power of attorney to get involved in making these decisions. If your parent is considered competent, his or her decision is the final choice – even if you believe it's unsafe or risky.

When your parent is competent to make decisions in his/her best interest, there are three main principles to follow when discussing where he/she should live and how safe they are:

1) **Respect your parent's autonomy:** it is his or her right to choose and make his or her own decisions.
2) **Obtain your parent's informed consent:** your parent must understand and agree to any of the changes you make to his or her living arrangements. You should also prepare any disagreements and for your parent to change their consent.
3) **Understand your parent's definition of "quality of life":** you understand what brings meaning and purpose in your parent's life, what his or her values are, what is comfortable and familiar to them, and what supports his or her sense of well-being. (This may not match your definition!)

Your parent's definition of quality of life is a very complex consideration. Frequently your idea or your siblings' idea of where your parent should live so that he or she remains safe and adequately cared for is different from your aging parent's.

Always keep in mind that your parent has standards of living that have been developed and defined prior to any impairment he or she may now be experiencing. Be sure to know what those are. Be cautious not to impose your own standards on your parent.

What is familiar and what holds meaning or purpose for your parent will in part determine where he or she wants to live. Keep in mind that the current living arrangement is familiar and your parent has established routines and special connections around this setting. If you change this, there must be a very good reason or the change can and will disrupt your parent's sense of well-being.

Questionnaire #10: Identifying the Right Level of Care for Your Parent

It's important to note that the least restrictive environment is the best option for your aging parent. "Least restrictive environment" means a living arrangement in which your parent can be safely maintained and their quality of life can be upheld.

Be careful to match the needs, wants, and personality of your aging parent. Take time to get to know who your parent is now—their wants, ideas, and needs may change as they grow older and become more vulnerable.

There are many housing options to choose from, including good options for parents who can no longer live in their own homes. When moving an aging parent into a facility, be mindful that there are rules and regulations. You're entering a business environment, not your parent's personal home. When it's their home, it's their rules. But outside of their home, the rules are no longer theirs to make. When you have no other options, don't leave your loved one to suffer through that alone.

The questionnaires in this section will help you assess whether or not it makes sense for them to move out of their home and into a different living situation. These are the possible living arrangement options:

- **Hospital:** This is a temporary living situation due to illness that requires the acute care of medical staff; they may also need to be in rehab to gain back strength and endurance.
- **Nursing Facilities:** This is long-term care in a setting that is medically required for the elderly parent who needs more specialized care.
- **Assisted living centers and adult residential facilities:**
  - Small settings that are like a home ("Board and Care")
  - Large facilities that house a continuum of care ranging from independent, supervisory care, personal care, and directed care.

- **Retirement communities:** Though these can be daunting to move into, retirement communities are an option that can bring more vibrant living to the elderly in a way that's more accessible for them. These communities offer entertainment and activities that support the aging population.

 Remember: The only reason to move your parent from their home is if they can no longer meet their lifestyle goals and they want and need to have more access to socialization and support.

- **Home:** There is no place like home and keeping your parent safe with his/her needs met can be accomplished with in-home companion care, private duty nursing, and monitoring services (which include cameras).

Instructions for Using Living Arrangement Assessment Questionnaires

1) Before you begin, review your assessment sheets; these will help clarify what type of assistance your parent needs
2) Read each statement or question in each category and check only the statements *that are almost always true*.
3) Read each category until you have come to the category that describes your parent's current level of functioning.
4) When you have reached the right category, stop and review the action plan to see what your parent's living arrangement options are.

1) Hospital

☑ **Check** any statement that is *almost always true* of your parent.
- ☐ Your parent currently needs medical attention or treatment only available in a hospital.
- ☐ Your parent is currently mentally unstable to the extent of being a danger to himself or others.

If you checked either of these statements, STOP!
Review the action information that follows.

> **ACTION:**
> - Your parent most likely needs to be hospitalized or treated within a medical care setting until your parent's condition is stabilized.
> - Call your parent's physician immediately.
> - This level of care will most likely be temporary.
> - Once your parent is medically stabilized, reevaluate his/her current level of functioning.
> - Since your parent has been under the direct care of healthcare staff, ask what level of care they recommend.
> - Work with a medical social worker to identify the best level of care for your parent at this time.
> - Check to see if this level of care is a temporary need or if your parent requires a recommendation for permanent living arrangements.

If you have not located the appropriate living arrangement for your parent, continue to the next questionnaire.

2) Nursing Facilities (Extended Care Facilities)

☑ **Check** any statement that is ***almost always true*** of your parent.
   - ☐ Your parent is disoriented all the time.
   - ☐ Your parent is immobile and always requires assistance to perform basic daily living tasks, such as transferring from bed to chair, feeding self, bathing, dressing, taking medication or treatments.
   - ☐ Your parent has special therapy needs that he/she cannot manage without 24-hour nursing assistance.
   - ☐ Your parent requires total care for all their basic daily living needs and has special treatment procedures on a daily basis that he/she cannot perform.

☐ Your parent requires total care because he/she is bedridden and cannot perform any of their special medical treatments without full assistance from a nurse.

☐ Your parent requires special therapies, i.e. complex diet, complex medical or close monitoring to be compliant with treatment due to their inability to perform or understand. *(This does not include your parent refusing to comply with treatment they need.)*

If you checked either of these statements, STOP! Review the action information that follows.

ACTION:
- Your parent may be a candidate for Nursing Care Facility: Skilled Nursing Unit placement.
- If you feel your parent needs this level of care, your parent's physician will need to become actively involved.
- The physician may also recommend that a professionally trained individual (generally a social worker) assist in placing your parent in an appropriate setting.

If you have not located the appropriate living arrangement for your parent, continue to the next questionnaire.

3) Assisted Living Centers & Facilities

These facilities are licensed housing arrangements that are staffed with personnel competent to provide the residents their needed care. They generally provide apartments, semi-private, or private bedrooms along with 24-hour supervision so your parent's needs are always addressed regardless of time of day.

☑ Check any statement that is **_almost always true_** of your parent.

☐ Your parent has intermittent periods of disorientation.

☐ Your parent wanders around the home and out into the community without being aware of where he or she is.

☐ Your parent's ability to perform daily living tasks fluctuates with not being able to safely manage to not managing at all.

☐ Your parent requires supervision all the time to remain safe.

☐ Your parent has difficulty feeding him or herself.

☐ Your parent needs assistance to bathe safely.

☐ Your parent needs assistance dressing and undressing.

☐ Your parent needs assistance with toileting.

☐ Your parent needs assistance getting in and out of bed/chair.

☐ Your parent needs assistance managing their medication schedule *(he or she does not routinely remember pills or medication).*

☐ Your parent relies on others to perform more complex tasks of living independently, i.e. shopping, cooking, transportation, laundry, housekeeping, financial/bill management, and is unable to perform daily living activities, such as bathing, dressing, transferring without assistance, toileting, and eating.

If you checked either of these statements, STOP! Review the action information that follows.

ACTION:

Your parent may be a candidate for assisted living facilities or centers. There are several levels of care in these centers that can meet your parent's care and safety needs.

- If you choose an assisted living facility, your parent's needs can be directly met by a 24-hour staff.
- If this is the level of care your parent may need, it may be more cost-effective to consider a live-in person or two 12-hour, in-home, private duty aides.
- This is costly, but it may be the best arrangement for your parent, or if there are no assisted living facilities or residential care homes in your community.

If you have not located the appropriate living arrangement for your parent, continue to the next questionnaire.

4) Retirement Community Living

☑ **Check** any statement that is *almost always true* of your parent.

- ☐ Your parent has intermittent periods of disorientation.
- ☐ Your parent is socially isolated (friends no longer can easily meet or spend time together).
- ☐ Your parent needs help maintaining the home and/or yard.
- ☐ Your parent needs help getting at least one good meal per day.
- ☐ Your parent cannot drive safely any longer and needs assistance getting out to do necessary tasks, such as shopping, appointments, banking, and socializing.
- ☐ Your parent wants to downsize or move to an age-segregated community.

If you checked either of these statements, STOP! Review the action information that follows.

> **ACTION:**
>
> An alternative living arrangement to remaining in their own home would be retirement community living. Within these communities, minimal assistance can be provided by:
>
> - A private-pay companion 1 to 2 times per week for 4-8 hours each time.
> - Community resources such as the Area Agency on Aging, which may be available to recommend the support needed.

If you have not located the appropriate living arrangement for your parent, continue to the next questionnaire.

5) Parent's Home

Part 1:

☑ **Check** the statement if your parent can perform the following tasks without assistance:

- ☐ Your parent can ambulate and transfer from bed to chair to bed without assistance.
- ☐ Your parent can manage his or her own toileting needs.
- ☐ Your parent can manage to call 911 or medical intervention when needed (*Emergency Response System*).

Part 2:

☑ **Check** the statement if your parent needs help with any of the following:

- ☐ Your parent needs help with cooking a main meal but can manage to prepare a snack.
- ☐ Your parent is not eating a well-balanced diet because it is too difficult to plan and prepare.
- ☐ Your parent cannot drive safely any longer and needs assistance getting out to do necessary tasks, such as shopping, appointments, banking, and socializing.

- [ ] Your parent does not keep up with personal hygiene anymore because he or she is afraid or too tired to accomplish the necessary tasks
- [ ] Your parent's clothing is unclean or are ragged.
- [ ] Your parent cannot remember to take medication or keep medication organized to take properly.
- [ ] Your parent gets confused at times and may not safely perform necessary daily tasks.

If you checked all the statements in Part 1 or Part 2, STOP!
Review the action information that follows.

ACTION:
- Your parent is still able to remain in his own home safely, with adequate assistance provided.
- Your parent will need a minimum of 4 to 8 hours of daily support to meet his or her needs.
- There are alternatives to remaining in the home with assistance, provided your community has these programs:
    - Assisted living apartment communities
    - Adult day-care programs with services like transportation to shopping and doctor appointments, security, recreational activities, and medication reminders.

At this point, you have hopefully identified the right level of care for your aging parent. If you are still unsure, you need to consult with a professional. A geriatric care manager or a social worker who has specialized in gerontology would be the best choices.

3

Developing an Action Plan

IN THIS CHAPTER:

- **Instructions on Developing an Action Plan**
- **Role of a Geriatric Care Manager**
- **Functional Assessment**
- **Neurocognitive Assessment**
- **Emotional Assessment**
- **Depression Assessment**
- **Spirituality Assessment**
- **Behavioral and Social Assessment**
- **Living Arrangements for Your Aging Parent**

You are now ready to develop your plan of action on how to assist your parent to meet his or her current needs. Request that all available family members meet together to discuss the data you have gathered.

Instructions on Developing an Action Plan:

1) Designate one person to lead the discussion, ask questions, and compile the answers on the blank Action Plan sheets that follow. If it is too difficult to select a family member to take this leadership role, ask a geriatric care manager or social worker to help facilitate this family meeting. At this point of the action planning, it is recommended to involve a Geriatric Care Manager for assistance in finalizing the action plan.

2) Together, review your assessment sheets for each section.

3) Based on the data from each assessment section, you need to decide if it is time to get involved in assisting your parent.

4) If you determine that it is, discuss who will be available to provide this help.

5) List all the people you believe are available to help.

Family who can help:

_____   _____

_____   _____

_____   _____

Friends who can help:

_____   _____

_____   _____

_____   _____

Hired caregivers who can help:

_____   _____

_____   _____

Geriatric Care Managers:

_____   _____

What is the Role of a Geriatric Care Manager

These professionals can facilitate discussions on difficult topics and complex issues. Organizations like the Aging Life Care Association (1-520-881-8008, www.aginglifecare.org) or the Eldercare Locator (1-800-677-1116) can help you find a geriatric care manager near your family member's residence. Additionally, support groups for age-related conditions may recommend geriatric care managers who have aided other families in similar situations.

The cost of Geriatric Care Managers varies and may be expensive, but depending on your family circumstances, they offer a useful service to help you and your family members navigate the winding Roadmap of Parent Care for your aging parent. Most Geriatric Care Managers charge by the hour, and more than likely, you will have to pay for this service out-of-pocket as Medicare and most insurance plans do not pay for Geriatric Care Managers.

When interviewing a geriatric care manager, you might want to ask:

- Are you a licensed geriatric care manager?
- How long have you been providing care management services?
- Are you available for emergencies around the clock?
- Does your company provide home care services?
- How will you communicate information to me?
- What are your fees? Will you provide information on fees in writing prior to starting services?
- Can you provide references?

Now you are ready to complete your parent's Action Plan. Transfer the data from each assessment sheet from chapter 2 over to this Action Plan. Be sure to include who will be responsible for ensuring the Action Plan is carried out.

Remember this Action Plan is just the beginning. Things change and so will your parent's needs and your ability to be the caregiver. If you find some part of the plan is not working, go back and reevaluate to find out what has changed. As these changes occur, be sure to alert everyone who needs to know.

Functional Assessment

List all information regarding your parent's ability to handle activities of daily living, as well as their ability to handle more complex tasks of independent living. Include any observations from the questionnaires on pages 35-39:

_____

_____

Action Plan: Functional Assessment

Once you have an understanding of how your parent is functioning in each of these areas, you need to determine how best to help them. Identify what level of care is needed and locate the resources available to support these needs.

- In-Home Care Agencies can offer support that may be needed. Be sure to investigate any agency and caregivers you plan to hire.
- Select one of your family members to review the status of any In-Home Care Agency you may want to hire: information can be obtained thru the State Licensing Department for Home Care services.
- Regardless of who you choose to select the appropriate In-Home Care Agency, they will need to evaluate the agency's services, costs, and the caregivers providing those services. It must be noted that In-Home Care agencies can differ in costs, quality of care, caregiver training, and supervision of caregivers in your aging parent's home. Thoroughly investigate and ask questions to determine if an agency is the right fit for your parent's home and daily life. If this task is too daunting, contact a Geriatric Care Manager. They can offer assistance with identifying and determining whether an In-Home Care Agency can meet your aging parent's level of care needs in the home. Working on behalf of your parent, they can provide the monitoring and supervision of this agency and their staff to assure they are meeting your parents needs. Often they will introduce the caregivers initial visit to your parent's home and provide an orientation of your parent's individualized plan of care.

```
┌─────────────────────────────────────────────────────────────┐
│  Your Action Plan:                                          │
│  _____│
│                                                             │
│  _____│
│                                                             │
│  _____│
│                                                             │
│  _____│
│                                                             │
│  _____│
│                                                             │
│  _____│
│                                                             │
└─────────────────────────────────────────────────────────────┘
```

Of the people you identified on page 64, list the names of who can help and who will ensure this action plan is completed:

_____   _____

_____   _____

Neurocognitive Assessment

Neurocognitive Signs and Symptoms

List changes/symptoms. Include observations from questionnaire on page 41-42:

_____

_____

_____

_____

_____

_____

_____

_____

_____

Action Plan: Neurocognitive Assessment

If you have checked any of the statements in this section, consult with your parent's primary care physician immediately.

- Select one of the primary caregivers (*preferably the family member who is the Medical Power of Attorney or professional GCM*) to communicate these observations to your aging parent's physician and/or any specialists that are currently treating your parent. (There are important treatment concerns that only the physicians can determine).
- Be sure to support your parent in communicating frankly with the physician.

Your Action Plan:

_____

_____

_____

_____

_____

_____

Of the people you identified on page 64, list the names of who can help and who will ensure this action plan is completed:

_____   _____

_____   _____

Emotional Assessment

List changes/symptoms. Include observations from questionnaire on pages 43-44:

_____

_____

_____

Action Plan: Emotional Assessment

If you have checked any of the statements in this section, consult with your parent's primary care physician immediately.

- Select one of the primary caregivers (*preferably the family member who is the Medical Power of Attorney or professional GCM*) to communicate these observations to your aging parent's physician and/or any specialists that are currently treating your parent. (There are important treatment concerns that only the physicians can determine).
- Be sure to support your parent in communicating frankly with the physician.

Your Action Plan:

_____

_____

_____

_____

_____

Of the people you identified on page 64, list the names of who can help and who will ensure this action plan is completed:

_____   _____

_____   _____

Depression Assessment

List changes/symptoms. Include observations from questionnaire on pages 44-45, and the Geriatric Depression Scale on page 46:

_____

_____

_____

Action Plan: Emotional Assessment

If you have checked any of the statements in this section, consult with your parent's primary care physician immediately.

- Select one of the primary caregivers (preferably the family member who is the Medical Power of Attorney or professional GCM) to communicate these observations to your aging parent's physician and/or any specialists that are currently treating your parent (There are important treatment concerns that only the physicians can determine).
- Be sure to support your parent in communicating frankly with the physician.

Your Action Plan:

_____

_____

_____

_____

_____

_____

Of the people you identified on page 64, list the names of who can help and who will ensure this action plan is completed:

_____   _____

_____   _____

Spirituality Assessment

List observations about your parent's spiritual needs. Include observations from questionnaires on pages 47-50:

_____

_____

_____

Action Plan: Spirituality Assessment

- Select a Family member to address this arena of your aging parents life. Sometimes a friend can also assist with this.
- If you believe that your parent needs attention in connecting to their spirituality, contact your parent's spiritual leader to enlist their help in meeting your parent's spiritual needs.

✍ Note:

The key is to actively engage in assisting your parent in this area.

Remember, this is all about your understanding of your parent's spirituality, not what you want them to believe in or your spirituality.

Your Action Plan:

_____

_____

_____

_____

_____

_____

Of the people you identified on page 64, list the names of who can help and who will ensure this action plan is completed:

_____   _____

_____   _____

Behavioral and Social Assessment

List observations about your parent's spiritual needs. Include observations from questionnaires on pages 51-53:

_____

_____

_____

Action Plan: Behavioral and Social Assessment

These observations are warning signs, so if you have any of these statements, you need to consult with your parent's primary care physician, geriatric care manager, or geriatric psychologist, or request a referral to a neurologist.

- Select a family member preferably the Medical Power of Attorney to discuss these concerns and observations with your aging parent's physician.
- Request a referral to the appropriate specialist for an evaluation and determine what treatment may be in the best interest of your parent.

Your Action Plan:

_____

_____

_____

_____

_____

_____

Of the people you identified on page 64, list the names of who can help and who will ensure this action plan is completed:

_____   _____

_____   _____

Living Arrangements for Your Aging Parent

List the observations you have identified in the following areas. Be sure to include any information collected from the questionnaires (on pages 55 -62) utilized in each area.

Where should your parent live? What category does your parent fall under?

_____

_____

_____

_____

_____

_____

What alternative living arrangements are available or recommended?

_____

_____

Are any of these options feasible? ☐ Yes ☐ No   If yes, which ones?

_____

_____

✍ Notes: Living Arrangements for Your Aging Parent

You and your family are ready to develop an action plan to identify the best living arrangement for your parent.

If both of your parents are still living but only one is impaired, the decision to adjust their living arrangements must include the functioning spouse.

Keep in mind the cost and the impact any changes will have on the functioning spouse.

You will need his/her acceptance of the needs of his/her impaired spouse and of how to manage this in the best interest of both.

At this point of the action planning, a Geriatric Care Manager is recommended to help finalize this action plan.

Your Action Plan:

_____

_____

_____

_____

_____

Of the people you identified on page 64, list the names of who can help and who will ensure this action plan is completed:

_____   _____

_____   _____

The Definitive Guide to Providing Effective, Loving Care for Your Aging Parent

4

Gathering Personal Information

IN THIS CHAPTER:

- **Personal Medical Information**
- **All Important Document Locator**
- **About Advance Directives**
- **Power of Attorney Documents & Living Will**
- **Personal Insurance Information**
- **Medical & Important Healthcare Information**
- **Geriatric Physicians**
- **Questionnaire: Finding the Right Doctor**
- **Medical History & Physical Information Form**
- **Questionnaire: Allergies & Adverse Reactions**
- **Preparing for a Medical Office Visit**
- **Questionnaire: About Prescription Medications**
- **Inventory Sheets**
- **Questionnaire: Parent's Current Financial Resources**
- **Questionnaires: Attorney & Legal Documents**
- **Important Financial Contacts Form & Financial Assessment**
- **Inventory Income & Expenses - Liabilities & Assets Sheets**

This chapter is designed to help you organize your parent's personal, medical, legal, and financial information. The forms and information included in this chapter can help you identify and locate important documents to assist you in caring for your aging parent.

How to obtain the original and copies of your parent's Advance Directives are also included in this chapter. You may even be inspired to establish your own personal set of Advance Directives while you are doing them with your parent.

Personal Medical Information

- Advance Directives:
  - Health Care (Medical) Power of Attorney
  - Living Will
  - Pre-Hospital Advance Directive
  - Mental Health Power of Attorney
- Medical Information: What You Need to Know
  - Questionnaire – Does your Parent Have the Right Physician?
  - List of Important Physicians, Specialists, and Healthcare Professionals
  - Questionnaire – Medical History and Physical Information Form
  - Questionnaire – Allergies and Adverse Reactions
  - Inventory Sheets – Prescription Medications, Over the Counter Medications, and Vitamins/Herbals
  - Medical Office Visit – What You Need to Know
  - Preparing for a Medical Office Visit Form
  - Medical Insurances Information: Type and Policy

Current Legal Resources

- Questionnaire – Who are your Parent's Legal and Financial Resources?
- Questionnaire – Do you have the Right Attorney for your Parent?
- Questionnaire – Legal Documents – Where are they Located?

Personal Financial Information

- Financial Assessment
- Who are the Financial Contacts?
- Inventory Sheets
  - Income
  - Expenses
  - Assets
  - Liabilities
  - Lists of valuables: Description/Photos

All Important Document Locator

Please take the time to gather all this information. You may need to get signed permission from your parents to have this confidential and critical information.

1. If you need to create these documents, please do so using the format presented in this section.
2. Fill in as much as you can.
3. Ask your parent to inform their attorney and financial advisors that you need access to this information in order to provide the necessary support and assistance when needed.
4. If they do not have an attorney, assist them in obtaining one.
5. Bring them to their bank to establish your role.

Once you have compiled this information keep these forms readily accessible so you know where to go or who to call to get what you need.

Find Advance Directives Forms by State

This section is designed to help you and your aging parent prepare their advance directives to reflect their individual health choices.

A helpful resource to review can be found at this website: *https://www.caringinfo.org/planning/advance-directives/*. From there, locate the link for "state-approved advanced directive documents" and then choose the appropriate state(s) from the drop-down menu.

One state's advance directive does not always work in another state. Some states will honor advance directives from another state while others will honor out-of-state advance directives only if they are similar to their state's own law. Additionally, some states do not have clear policies regarding the recognition of out-of-state advance directives. The best solution is if you spend a significant amount of time in more than one state, you should complete the advance directives for each state.

The PDFs may be filled in online, and some states allow online notarization. The forms should be saved and stored digitally, as well as printed so that they may be formalized by witness signatures or notarized if your state so requires. States vary in their requirements for witnesses, notarization, and other specifics so be sure to review the form and its instructions carefully.

What You Need to Know About Advance Directives

Every adult should have an advance directive that explains the type of healthcare they do or do not want when they can't make their own decisions. Your parent should also appoint someone who can speak for them to make sure their wishes are carried out.

What are the Advance Directive Documents?
- Healthcare Power of Attorney (Medical Power of Attorney)
- Living Will
- Mental Health Power of Attorney
- Pre-Hospital Advance Directive

What is a Healthcare Power of Attorney?
If your parent does not have a Healthcare Power of Attorney form filled out already, take the time to explain what it is and why it's important for them to appoint someone. You could say:
- "A Healthcare Power of Attorney (or Medical Power of Attorney) is a legal document that appoints a person to become your 'surrogate' if you become incapacitated and unable to physically or mentally manage your affairs."
- "The Healthcare Power of Attorney document gives the person you choose the legal authority to talk to your doctors, manage your medical care, and make medical decisions for you if you can't."

Remind your parent that the best choice for this role should be someone they believe:
- Will follow their wishes.
- Lives nearby enough to be with them when needed and is willing to help if a crisis occurs.

- Has the physical and mental ability to assist in making healthcare decisions when your aging parent cannot.
- Has the tenacity to be persistent with providers and be the 'squeaky wheel' if needed.

What is a Living Will?

If your parent does not already have a living will, take the time to explain what it is and why it is important for them to have one.

A living will is a written, legally binding document that informs your aging parent's doctors about his/her preferences for medical care at the end of life. Because these are legal documents, you may use a lawyer to help your parent understand and write a living will.

As an alternative to utilizing a lawyer, a living will can be written with a social worker or even by yourself with a little research. However, this document will require a lot of thought and is best done in concert with a professional.

Every state has different laws and practices, so please be sure to use a living will that your state recognizes. Some use standard forms, while others allow you to draft your own.

Be sure to follow your state's rules about what kind of witnesses you must use and whether the document needs to be notarized.

What is a Mental Health Power of Attorney?

Like a medical advance directive or a healthcare power of attorney, a Psychiatric Advance Directive is a legal document completed in a time of wellness that provides instructions regarding treatment or services your parent wishes to have (or not have) during a mental health crisis.

- A mental health crisis is when a person is unable to make or communicate rational decisions.

- A Mental Health Power of Attorney allows your parent to specify considerations about their mental health care treatment and appoint a person who will make decisions about their treatment in the event of a mental health crisis.

Be sure to check with your state for the correct documents and the criteria to enact it, and confirm that your state accepts this advance directive.

What is a Pre-Hospital Advance Directive (Do Not Resuscitate-DNR) Form?

This is an official document signed by a medical professional and your aging parent. The purpose of this document is to inform EMS personnel about a patient's decision to forgo resuscitative actions.

Be sure to check with your state for the correct documents and the criteria to enact it, and confirm that your state accepts this advance directive.

Other Notes on Powers of Attorney

A power of attorney names a person who can act on your parent's behalf; this person is called an "agent" or "attorney-in-fact".

- Some states recognize "springing" powers of attorney, which means the agent can start using it only once your parent is incapacitated.
- Some states do not, which means the day the durable power of attorney is signed, the agent can use the document.

To find out your state's directives, look for the link on this page: *https://www.caringinfo.org/planning/advance-directives/*

General powers of attorney give the agent broad authority. They can step into your parent's shoes and handle all their medical, legal, and financial affairs until your parent becomes mentally incapacitated.

Durable powers of attorney may be limited, or may give the agent broad authority to handle all your parent's medical, legal and financial affairs.

- The agent keeps the authority even if your parent becomes physically or mentally incapacitated.
- This means that your family may not have to ask for a court to intervene if you have a medical crisis or severe cognitive decline such as late-stage dementia.
- Sometimes, medical decision-making is included in a durable power of attorney for healthcare.

Personal Information Form

Fill in all relevant information about your parent.

Name: _____ Date of Birth (DOB): _____

Address: _____

Phone number: _____ SS #: _____

Medical Information

Medicare number: _____

Secondary insurance: _____

Policy number: _____

Military ID number: _____

Driver's License number: _____

Emergency contact person: _____

Relationship: _____

Address: _____

Phone: _____

Doctor (primary care physician): _____

Address: _____

Phone: _____

Hospital: _____

Address: _____

Phone _____

Medical Power of Attorney: _____

Address: _____

Phone: _____

Financial Power of Attorney:

Address: _____

Phone: _____

Fiduciary (if applicable): _____

Title: _____

Address: _____

Phone: _____

Family/friends:
(*Other family members or friends to notify in case of emergency*)

Name: _____ Phone:_____

Address:_____

Name: _____ Phone:_____

Address:_____

Name: _____ Phone:_____

Address:_____

Name: _____ Phone:_____

Address:_____

Name: _____ Phone:_____

Address:_____

Personal Insurance Information

Life Insurance Company: _____

Type of policy _____ Policy #_____ Face value _____

Address of company _____Phone _____

Agent _____ Phone _____Fax _____

Life Insurance Company: _____

Type of policy _____ Policy #_____ Face value _____

Address of company _____Phone _____

Agent _____ Phone _____Fax _____

Burial insurance _____ Carrier _____

Policy # _____Address of company _____

Agent _____ Phone _____Fax _____

Auto insurance carrier _____

Policy #_____ Address of company _____

Agent_____ Phone_____Fax _____

Homeowner's insurance carrier _____Policy # _____

Paid with mortgage _____ Paid by homeowner _____

Address of company _____

Agent_____ Phone _____Fax _____

Other insurance_____ Carrier _____

Policy # _____ Address of company _____

Agent _____ Phone _____Fax _____

Other insurance_____ Carrier_____

Policy #_____Address of company _____

Agent_____ Phone_____Fax _____

Medical Information

You will use this medical information section frequently as you provide help and care for your parent. Keep a copy in a separate envelope, ready to accompany your parent to a doctor's appointment or to the hospital.

Important Physician and Specialist Information
Emergency Phone # 911

Hospital _____

Address _____

Phone _____ Website_____

Primary care physician (PCP)_____

Address _____

Phone _____ Website_____

Cardiologist _____

Address _____

Phone _____ Website_____

Pulmonary specialist _____

Address _____

Phone _____ Website_____

Surgeon_____

Address _____

Phone _____ Website_____

Dentist _____

Address _____

Phone _____ Website _____

Optometrist _____

Address _____

Phone _____ Website _____

Audiologists _____

Address _____

Phone _____ Website _____

Other specialist _____

Address _____

Phone _____ Website _____

Specialty _____

Address _____

Phone _____ Website _____

Pharmacy _____

Address _____

Phone _____ Website _____

Additional Important Healthcare Information

Home Health Agency

Name _____

Address _____

Phone _____ Website _____

Contact person _____

Therapists

Physical Therapist _____

Address _____

Phone _____ Website_____

Occupational Therapist

Name _____

Address _____

Phone _____ Website_____

Social worker

Name _____

Address _____

Phone _____ Website_____

Dietitian

Name _____

Address _____

Phone _____ Website_____

Other Specialists

Name _____

Specialty _____

Address _____

Phone _____ Website_____

Name_____

Specialty _____

Address _____

Phone _____ Website_____

Name_____

Specialty _____

Address _____

Phone _____ Website_____

Geriatric Physicians: What You Need to Know

Use this list of characteristics as a guide if you are looking for a new physician for your parent. If you and your parent feel comfortable with your parent's present physician, it is not necessary to change doctors just because they're not a geriatric physician. You can encourage your present physician to STOP rushing, LOOK closely, and LISTEN to your parent while they are treating them.

Geriatric Physicians:

- Specialize in the medical problems of older adults.
- Approach their elderly patients from the social as well as the medical perspective.
- Are trained to understand what is physically normal for older adults.
- Are trained NOT to overlook a treatable disease because the symptoms are considered normal aging.
- Do NOT read pathology into what is normal aging.
- Work collaboratively with other disciplines:
  - Geriatric care managers
  - Social workers
  - Physical therapists

- Dietitians
- Occupational therapists
- Speech therapists
- Neuropsychologists
- Nurse practitioners
- Tend to spend more time listening to the elderly patient.
- Look at the emotional, mental, and social impact of an illness, and don't focus only on the physical symptoms.

Questionnaire #11: Is this the Right Doctor for Your Parent?

Here is a list of questions to ask either your parent's current doctor or your parent about the current doctor's attitude and practice.

Attitude

Yes No

☐ ☐ Does the doctor engage in conversation and not make you or your parent feel rushed?

☐ ☐ Does the doctor allow time for follow-up questions?

☐ ☐ Does the doctor listen to your parent and answer questions?

☐ ☐ Can your parent talk openly to the doctor about personal concerns?

☐ ☐ Is the doctor clear when they talk about cause and treatment?

☐ ☐ Does the doctor treat both you and your parent with respect?

Practice

Yes No

☐ ☐ Does the doctor try to discover the origin of the problem rather than just prescribing a drug for the symptom?

☐ ☐ Does the doctor have an associate to whom you can turn to if he or she is unavailable?

☐ ☐	Does the doctor understand your parent's view and preferences on surgery, transfusions, and life support?
☐ ☐	Does the doctor or their staff return phone calls in a timely manner?
☐ ☐	Is the front office staff friendly and available?

> ✍ **NOTE:**
> If you have checked any NOs, you may want to help your parent find a new doctor.

Questionnaire #12: Medical History and Physical Information Form

This form has typical questions you will be asked when your parent schedules with a new doctor. If you complete this with your parent at home, you will be familiar enough with their medical history to easily complete the form in the doctor's office. This will also help you gain a better knowledge about your parent's past and present health.

Family History:

Have you or any family member been diagnosed with:

	Yes	No	Who
Cancer	☐	☐	_____
Tuberculosis	☐	☐	_____
Diabetes	☐	☐	_____
Stroke	☐	☐	_____
Epilepsy	☐	☐	_____
Mental illness	☐	☐	_____
Thyroid condition	☐	☐	_____
Poor circulation	☐	☐	_____
Prostate problems	☐	☐	_____
Kidney stones	☐	☐	_____

Arthritis	☐	☐	_____
Stomach ulcers	☐	☐	_____
Diverticulitis	☐	☐	_____

Surgeries:

Type_____ Date_____

Type _____ Date_____

Type _____ Date_____

Habits:

Do you smoke?   Yes ☐   No ☐   How many packs per day? _____

Do you drink?   Yes ☐   No ☐

How many drinks per day? _____   Week? _____

Symptoms:

	Past	Present
Eye, Ear, Nose, and Throat		
Headaches	☐	☐
Dizziness or fainting spells	☐	☐
Blurred vision	☐	☐
Double vision	☐	☐
Infected eyes	☐	☐
Pain behind eyes	☐	☐
Earaches	☐	☐
Ringing in ears	☐	☐
Recurrent nose bleeds	☐	☐
Decrease in hearing	☐	☐
Sinus trouble	☐	☐
Difficulty swallowing	☐	☐
Circulatory, Respiratory, Digestive		
Chest pains	☐	☐
Night sweats	☐	☐
Shortness of breath	☐	☐
Purple fingers or lips	☐	☐

Heart flutters	☐	☐
High blood pressure	☐	☐
Swelling of hands, feet, or ankles	☐	☐
Recurrent stomach pains	☐	☐
Belching or heartburn	☐	☐
Nausea and vomiting	☐	☐
Vomiting blood	☐	☐
Abdominal cramping	☐	☐
Blood in stool	☐	☐

Difficulties with Urination

Pain	☐	☐
Frequent	☐	☐
Up at night	☐	☐
Hard to start	☐	☐
Blood	☐	☐
Loss of urine when cough or sneeze	☐	☐
Backaches or back pains	☐	☐

Orthopedic

Joint pains	☐	☐
Swelling of joints	☐	☐
Muscle spasms or cramps	☐	☐
Loss of sensation in extremities	☐	☐
Trembling of extremities	☐	☐

Endocrine

Growth in neck or throat	☐	☐
Tiredness without apparent cause	☐	☐
Easy bruising	☐	☐
Skin rash	☐	☐

Date of last physical exam _____

Date of last pap smear _____

Date of last EKG _____

Date of last radiation _____

Date of last chemo _____

Questionnaire #13: Allergies and Adverse Reactions

To Medications:

Name of medication _____

Generic name _____

Description of reaction _____

Name of medication _____

Generic name _____

Description of reaction _____

Name of medication _____

Generic name _____

Description of reaction _____

To Foods:

Name of food_____

Description of reaction _____

Name of food_____

Description of reaction _____

To X-ray Dye:

Description of reaction _____

Reason for x-ray? _____

Approximate date this happened: _____

Medical Insurance Information Locator

Primary Health Insurance _____

Policy # _____

Address of company _____

Agent _____ Location of policy _____

Phone _____ Fax _____

Medicare Supplement Insurance _____

Policy # _____

Address of company _____

Agent _____ Location of policy _____

Phone _____ Fax _____

Long-term Care Insurance _____

Policy # _____

Address of company _____

Agent _____ Location of policy _____

Phone _____ Fax _____

Health Maintenance Organization (HMO) _____

Policy # _____

Address of company _____

Agent _____ Location of policy _____

Phone _____ Fax _____

Other Insurance Carrier _____

Policy # _____

Address of company _____

Agent _____ Location of policy _____

Phone _____ Fax _____

Preparing for a Medical Office Visit: What You Need to Know

It is helpful to be clear about what your parent has experienced since the last visit to their doctor. Often doctors are rushed and will not wait while the patient tries to remember what they want to talk about. With prompting from this completed form, your parent will remember what concerns they've had since the last visit.

As you complete this form or review what your parent has written, you can focus on their condition on a regular basis. Since the form is intended to be taken to the doctor, you can use it to record what the doctor said as well as any changes made in medication. Remember to record these changes on the "Inventory Sheet: Prescription Medications".

✍ **NOTE:**

Make several copies of the following "*Preparing for Medical Office Visit Form*". Leave a new form on the refrigerator, desk, wall, or wherever you or your parent can easily write down concerns to discuss with the doctor. Be sure to take the form to the doctor's visit with your parent.

Preparing for Medical Office Visit Form

Name of healthcare provider _____

Address _____ Phone _____

Concerns or observations since last appointment:

_____

_____

_____

Since my last appointment I have been feeling:

☐ About the same   ☐ Better   ☐ Worse

Since my last appointment I have been sleeping:

☐ About the same   ☐ Less than usual   ☐ More than usual

Since my last appointment I have been eating:

☐ About the same   ☐ Less than usual   ☐ More than usual

Since my last appointment my weight has:

Increased about _____ lbs.   Decreased about _____ lbs.

Physician's or other healthcare provider's recommendations:

_____

_____

Changes in medication

Eliminate these prescriptions: _____

_____

_____

Add these prescriptions: _____

_____

_____

Date & Time of Next Appointment: _____

Questionnaire #4: About Prescription Medications

Make copies of this blank sheet and take several with you for each doctor's visit. When your parent's doctor prescribes a new medication, ask the questions on this form.

Name of Drug Prescribed

Generic:_____

Brand name: _____

How and when should it be taken? _____

What does "take as needed" or "prn" mean? _____

Does it interact with any over-the-counter drugs?   ☐ Yes   ☐ No

If it does, what needs to be avoided? _____

_____

What should be done if a dose is missed? _____

Should this medication be taken?

     ☐ Before a meal   ☐ With a meal   ☐ After a meal

What should be avoided while taking this drug?

Foods_____

Drinks _____

Activities _____

What side effects should we watch for? _____

_____

Is it necessary to take the whole prescription?   ☐ Yes   ☐ No

Inventory Sheets

The following inventory sheets will help you, your parent, and the doctor keep track of the various medications your parent has been prescribed or currently takes.

They are good for reviewing your parent's medications to identify any potential duplications or interactions that may undermine the effectiveness of other drugs. Additionally, they can help identify times when generic alternatives can be used in place of name-brand medications.

Often several doctors are prescribing and one doctor, usually the primary care physician, needs to be aware of ALL medications, even over the counter and vitamin or herbal supplements. The doctor can use the following inventory sheets to get a clear and comprehensive look at what medication and drugs your parent takes.

ACTION:

- Make several copies of these inventory sheets and update regulary.
- If you accompany your parent to doctor visits, update the prescription inventory form at each visit.
- If you are not nearby, or don't need to accompany your parent to doctor visits, update these inventory sheets with your parent every three to four months.

Inventory Sheet: Prescription Medications

Name (brand or generic)_____

Rx# _____ Dosage _____

When taken_____

Reason for medication _____

Precautions _____

Where purchased _____ Phone _____

Number of refills _____ Date of refill _____

Name (brand or generic)_____

Rx# _____ Dosage _____

When taken_____

Reason for medication _____

Precautions _____

Where purchased _____ Phone _____

Number of refills _____ Date of refill _____

Name (brand or generic)_____

Rx# _____ Dosage _____

When taken_____

Reason for medication _____

Precautions _____

Where purchased _____ Phone _____

Number of refills _____ Date of refill _____

Name (brand or generic)_____

Rx# _____ Dosage _____

When taken_____

Reason for medication _____

Precautions _____

Where purchased _____ Phone _____

Number of refills _____ Date of refill _____

Inventory Sheet: Over-the-Counter Medications

Name of product _____

Reason to take this product_____

Direction on when to take it _____

Precautions _____

Name of product _____

Reason to take this product_____

Direction on when to take it _____

Precautions _____

Name of product _____

Reason to take this product_____

Direction on when to take it _____

Precautions _____

Name of product _____

Reason to take this product_____

Direction on when to take it _____

Precautions _____

Name of product _____

Reason to take this product_____

Direction on when to take it _____

Precautions _____

Name of product _____

Reason to take this product_____

Direction on when to take it _____

Precautions _____

Inventory Sheet: Vitamins/Herbals

Name of product _____

Brand_____ Dosage_____

Where purchased _____Phone _____

Direction on when to take it _____

Precautions _____

Name of product _____

Brand_____ Dosage_____

Where purchased _____Phone _____

Direction on when to take it _____

Precautions _____

Name of product _____

Brand_____ Dosage_____

Where purchased _____Phone _____

Direction on when to take it _____

Precautions _____

Name of product _____

Brand_____ Dosage_____

Where purchased _____Phone _____

Direction on when to take it _____

Precautions _____

Name of product _____

Brand_____ Dosage_____

Where purchased _____Phone _____

Direction on when to take it _____

Precautions _____

Questionnaire #15: Who are Your Parent's Current Legal and Financial Resources?

Who is the attorney currently representing your parent?

Name_____

Address _____

Phone _____Fax_____

Email_____ Website_____

Who is the accountant currently representing your parent?

Name_____

Address _____

Phone _____Fax_____

Email_____ Website_____

Who is currently doing the paperwork related to medical billing for your parent?

Name_____

Address _____

Phone _____Fax_____

Email_____ Website_____

✎ **NOTE:**

You may decide you need assistance reviewing medical bills, filing insurance claims, communicating to insurance companies, and appealing bills, etc. It is recommended you contact a geriatric care manager in your parent's community who can assist you in locating this type of service. You can obtain a list of geriatric care managers by contacting the Aging Life Care Association at 520-881-8008 (Tucson, AZ), Website: *www.aginglifecare.org*. Also, see chapter on Caregiver Resources.

Questionnaire #16: Is this the Attorney for your Parent?

Use this form to interview your parent's attorney or a potential attorney to ensure he or she is experienced in issues relevant to your parent.

- ☐ How many years have you been in practice?_____
- ☐ What is your specialty? _____
- ☐ Do you have experience in Elder Law?   ☐ Yes   ☐ No
- ☐ If you have Elder Law experience, what percentage of your practice do you estimate is in that area?   _____%
- ☐ Approximate number of Living Trusts and Durable Powers of Attorney you have prepared? _____
- ☐ Are you familiar with the laws that regulate long-term care issues and eligibility for Medicaid?   ☐ Yes   ☐ No
- ☐ Have you been involved in hearings and appeals related to Medicaid or Medicare?   ☐ Yes   ☐ No

---

✎ **NOTE:**
Even if you get positive answers on these questions, be sure to ask for and check references before hiring anyone.

Questionnaire #17: Regarding Legal Documents

The following questions are meant to focus your attention on several legal documents that need to be in place. If you answer "no" to any of these questions, discuss the advisability of having them with your parent and/or your parent's attorney. Does your parent have their Advance Directives in place?

Does your parent have a Durable Healthcare Power of Attorney?
(*Medical Power of Attorney*)   ☐ Yes   ☐ No

Do they have a Living Will?   ☐ Yes   ☐ No

If yes: Who has this authority? _____

Where is the document located? _____

If no: *Consider the advisability of this document and discuss with your parent and an attorney.*

Does your parent have a Mental Health Power of Attorney?   ☐ Yes   ☐ No

If yes: Who has this authority?

Where is the document located?

If no: *Consider the advisability of this document and discuss with your parent and an attorney.*

Does your parent have a Durable Power of Attorney document?

☐ Yes   ☐ No

If yes: Who has this authority? _____

Where is the document located? _____

If no: *Consider the advisability of this document and discuss with your parent and an attorney.*

Does your parent have a Living Trust?

☐ Yes   ☐ No   ☐ Revocable   ☐ Irrevocable

Who is the trustee(s) if your parent is or becomes incapacitated or incompetent?_____

Address _____

Phone _____ Email_____

Where is the document located? _____

If no: *Discuss the advantages and disadvantages with your parent and an attorney.*

Does your parent have an estate will?   ☐ Yes   ☐ No

If yes: Who is the executor of the will? _____

Address _____

Phone _____ Email_____

Where is the document located? _____

If no: *Discuss the advisability of having a will with your parent and an attorney.*

Important Financial Contacts

Attorney

Name_____

Address _____

Email _____

Phone _____ Fax _____

Financial Advisor

Name_____

Address _____

Email _____

Phone _____ Fax _____

Accountant

Name_____

Address _____

Email _____

Phone _____ Fax _____

Stockbroker

Name_____

Address _____

Email _____

Phone _____ Fax _____

Tax Preparer

Name_____

Address _____

Email _____

Phone _____ Fax _____

Banker

Name _____

Address _____

Email _____

Phone _____ Fax _____

Insurance Agent

Name _____

Address _____

Email _____

Phone _____ Fax _____

Other

Name _____

Address _____

Email _____

Phone _____ Fax _____

Financial Assessment

The following pages will help you identify what financial resources exist to support additional care, a higher level of care, or whatever other needs your parent has now or in the future.

It will also allow you to determine if your parent qualifies for a Medicaid program based on need.

Inventory Sheet: Income

This information will help you see what financial resources exist to support whatever needs your parent has now or in the future.

Income	Monthly	Annual
Social Security		
Pension		
Wages/Salary		
Interest		
Rental Income		
Dividends		
Loan Repayment		
Other		
Total		

Inventory Sheet: Expenses

This information will help you see how the financial resources are being used. It will also assist you in determining if there are any financial resources left over for additional care if needed.

Expenses	Monthly	Annual
Rent/Mortgage		
Taxes		
Income		
Property		
Utilities		
Phone		
Food		

Car Payment		
Gas		
Maintenance		
Home		
Car		
Insurance		
Health		
Long-term Care		
Life		
Property		
Car		
Other		
Medical		
Medication		
Equipment		
Entertainment		
Credit Card (total)		
Donations		
Other		
Total		

Inventory Sheet: Assets

If you are unable to get the approximate amount or value of the items listed below, at least list the account numbers and locations.

Assets	Location	Amount
Checking Accounts		
#		
#		
Savings Accounts		
#		
#		
Money Market Accounts		
#		
#		
Mutual Funds		
#		
#		
Bonds		
#		
#		
CDs		
#		
#		
Stocks		

Safe Deposit Box		
#		
Other Valuables		

Inventory Sheet: Liabilities

If you are unable to get the approximate amount or value of the items listed below, at least list the account numbers.

Liabilities		
Mortgage		
Carrier		
Address		Phone #
Approximate Amount $		
Personal Loans		
Carrier		Amount $
Carrier		Amount $
Credit Cards		
Type	Acct #	Balance $
Type	Acct #	Balance $
Type	Acct #	Balance $
Car Loan		
Carrier		
Address		Phone #
Balance $		
Other Obligations		
Description		$
Description		$
Property Taxes		
Payable to:		
Address:		
Approximate Amounts		$

Important Documents Locator

Medical and Health	Location
☐ Social Security card	_____
☐ Medicare card	_____
☐ HMO card	_____
☐ Life insurance policy	_____
☐ Medical supplement policy	_____
☐ Long-term care policy	_____
☐ Burial/funeral policy	_____
☐ Living Will	_____
☐ Medical Power of Attorney	_____
☐ Pre-Hospital Advance Directive	_____

Personal	Location
☐ Birth certificate	_____
☐ Marriage certificate	_____
☐ Divorce decree	_____
☐ Citizenship papers	_____
☐ Military discharge papers	_____
☐ Other	_____

Financial	Location
☐ Last year's tax return	_____
☐ Previous years' returns	_____
☐ Will	_____
☐ Trusts	_____
☐ Durable Power of Attorney	_____

- ☐ Credit cards   _____
- ☐ Previous month's bank statement   _____
- ☐ Annual award letter from Social Security _____
- ☐ Statement from retirement or pension plan _____
- ☐ Safety deposit box   _____

Property Information   Location

- ☐ Deed to house   _____
- ☐ Mortgage papers   _____
- ☐ Lease agreements   _____
- ☐ Automobile title   _____
- ☐ Other titles   _____

_____   _____

_____   _____

- ☐ Last property tax statement   _____
- ☐ Verification of homeowners' association fee _____
- ☐ Verification of mobile home lot rent   _____
- ☐ Homeowner's insurance   _____
- ☐ Auto insurance   _____
- ☐ Other insurance   _____

_____   _____

_____   _____

- ☐ Appraisal of valuables   _____

Document all valuables, furniture, vehicles, and any collections in the home. It is recommended to also document valuables with photographs. (*Use the pages in the Forms Workbook for added valuables as needed*)

Jewelry _____

_____

_____

Furniture _____

_____

_____

_____

_____

Art _____

_____

_____

_____

Vehicles _____

_____

_____

Collections _____

_____

_____

_____

✍ **NOTE: It is recommended to take photos of all valuables: jewelry, art, furniture, cars, and any collections in the home.**

5

Determining Living Arrangements

IN THIS CHAPTER:

- **Strategies for Staying at Home**
- **Checklist: Services**
- **Choosing In-Home Assistance for Your Parent**
- **Should Your Parent Move in with You?**
- **Questionnaire: For the Adult Child**
- **Questionnaire: For the Parent**
- **Continued Care Retirement Communities**
- **Checklist: Choosing an Assisted Living Facility**
- **Shared Housing**
- **Skilled Nursing Facilities**

Now that you have some idea of your parent's functional condition, mental and emotional behavior, and level of care needs, you will be able to make better decisions about their living arrangements. This chapter will review the various options and offer strategies for how to choose the best situation for your parent.

Basically, we all want to live in our own homes as long as possible. Your parent is no different. Their home is their sanctuary, the place they can be in control of who, how, what, and when to meet their needs.

The familiarity and comforts of home are undeniable. However, there are some drawbacks and concerns associated with aging in place.

One question to ask: *Is living in their own home in their best interest?*
If yes: Confirm that your parent's living situation includes proper home accommodations, a reliable support system, and a realistic assessment of their health status and abilities.

If no: You may need to find an alternative living arrangement, which can be stressful for everyone.

 The first step is to carefully evaluate the specific level of care your parent needs, and honestly assess whether that care can be feasibly delivered within their own home setting.

1. Caregiving responsibilities will often fall on the family who is available and willing to offer this support.
2. Needless to say, this can be a daunting experience if this is needed 24-hours daily.
3. You will need to talk about the realities and dangers of staying at home if your parent's health and or functional abilities are declining.

Strategies for Staying at Home

If your aging parent wants and can stay at home, you may need to adapt your parent's home to their changing needs to ensure their safety. Here are some key factors and strategies to consider.

Accessibility

Can your parent enter and exit the home without assistance? As it becomes more difficult for your parent to reach and bend, are the household items frequently used within easy reach?

Here are some ideas for making items more accessible:

If possible, purchase appliances that are more user-friendly:
- Side-by-side refrigerator
- Self-cleaning oven
- Cooktop with automatic shut off if pot becomes too hot
- Front controls on stove and range

If your parent uses a wheelchair, you may need to reorganize and renovate his/her living space:

- Most wheelchairs require 32-inch clearance through hallways and doorways
- Remove doors or replace with ones that have swing clear hinges
- Remove thresholds at doorways and install ramps wherever needed
- Lower counters
- Redesign the bathroom for wheelchair access

Mobility

If your parent lives in a multi-level residence:

- Install a chair lift on the stairs so he or she can move easily between floors
- Or rearrange so all necessary rooms (bedroom, bathroom, kitchen, living room) are on one floor

If your parent's mobility is extremely limited:

- Consolidate several necessary functions—cooking, dining, watching TV, or visiting with company—in one area (one room)

Safety

Being vulnerable to falls is another common problem your aging parent may have while living alone. Your parent's home needs to be free from physical hazards.

Here are some suggestions:

Remove:

- Scatter rugs
- Any furniture or lamps that can easily be knocked over
- Electric cords that are frayed or run across the floor
- Shag carpeting
- Slippery flooring
- Clutter in walkways

Clean:

- Clean and reorganize your parent's home and remove any obstacles.
- Clear out closets crammed with an accumulation of possessions.

To Increase Protection Against Fire:
- Install battery operated smoke alarms on or near the ceiling in the kitchen and the bedroom. *(Be sure these alarms are designed for the hearing-impaired—flashing light and sound)*

Lighting:
- Install non-glare lighting throughout the home.
- Make sure that the hallways and walk areas in and around the home are evenly lit.
- Use the highest allowable wattage bulbs in all light fixtures and lamps.
- Make sure that all rooms have a light near the door so that your parent will never walk into a dark room.
- Have a light switch or lamp by your parent's bed and by his/her favorite chair.

In the bathroom:
- Apply textured vinyl strips to the tub and shower floors or use non-slip mats.
- Do not use scatter rugs.
- Install grab bars beside your parent's tub, above the sink, and beside the toilet if necessary.
- Encourage your parent to use a long-handled scrubber for cleaning the tub, shower, sink, and toilets.

In the kitchen:
- Encourage your parent to wipe up all spills immediately.
- Be sure your parent uses only a sturdy step stool with handrails to reach higher places (recommend discouraging this practice).
- Provide long, lightweight tongs to reach for items.

Security - To keep your parent safe from crime:
- Check doors and windows to see if locks are adequate and in good repair.

- Consider installing an alarm system.
- Enroll in an emergency response system. This is a very good way of keeping your parent safe, as he or she can summon help quickly in can of a medical emergency. *(See Chapter 11, Caregiver Resources)*
- Install good lighting around the perimeter of the home so that anyone approaching the building is visible to neighbors and passersby.

Additional Safety Purchases:
- Raised toilet seats
- Handheld shower head
- Bedside commode for nighttime
- Night light in bedroom and bathroom
- Cordless phone
- Doorknobs with levers
- Telephone with large numbers
- Mediset for organizing weekly medications
- Non-breakable glasses and dinnerware

☑ Checklist: Services

Here is a list of services that your parent may need to remain at home or in the current living arrangement. Use this checklist to assist your parent in developing a safe and supportive in-home setting.

Need to Hire   **Who was Hired**

☐ Housecleaning   _____
    ☐ Once a Week
    ☐ Twice a Month
    ☐ Once a Month

☐ Laundry   _____
    ☐ Once a Week
    ☐ Twice a Month
    ☐ Once a Month

☐ Light House Cleaning   _____
    ☐ Change Bed Linens
    ☐ Dust, Vacuum
    ☐ Bathrooms, Kitchen

☐ Heavy Cleaning   _____
    ☐ Windows
    ☐ Floors
    ☐ All Fixtures: Lights, Fans, Etc.
    ☐ Appliances
    ☐ Baseboards
    ☐ Ceilings, Walls

☐ Yard Work   _____
    ☐ Front
    ☐ Back
    ☐ Patio
    ☐ Trim Trees

Need to Hire   **Who was Hired**

☐ Meal Preparation   _____
    ☐ Breakfast
    ☐ Lunch
    ☐ Dinner
    ☐ Other

☐ Meals on Wheels   _____

- ☐ Grocery Shopping   _____
  - ☐ Weekly
  - ☐ Twice a Month
  - ☐ Monthly
  - ☐ Delivery Service

- ☐ Transportation   _____
  - ☐ Physician Appointments
  - ☐ Shopping
  - ☐ Church
  - ☐ Errand Running
  - ☐ Recreation (e.g., senior center)
  - ☐ Other   _____

- ☐ Companionship   _____
  - ☐ Reading
  - ☐ Talking
  - ☐ Walking
  - ☐ Card Play, etc.

- ☐ Other   _____

Notes:_____

_____

_____

Choosing In-Home Assistance for Your Parent

Did you know that only approximately 20 percent of older people requiring care in the United States receive it in an institution? The rest are cared for by friends and family members or hired caregivers at home.

Choosing in-home assistance for your parent takes a lot of patience and critical thinking. When you invite someone into your parent's home you are giving that person your trust.

Be sure they deserve it! Do a background check.

If you are not available to personally oversee the quality and type of care being offered to your parent, hire a professional geriatric care manager or social worker to do it.

Questionnaire for Evaluating Agencies:

YES	NO	
☐	☐	Is the agency or independent contractor insured and bonded?
☐	☐	Are the caregivers supervised by the agency? Who pays for this? Agency / You *(circle one)*
☐	☐	Is there an assurance a caregiver will always be available?

How will the agency handle no-shows? _____

_____

_____

YES	NO	
☐	☐	Is the agency licensed? License number: _____
☐	☐	Does the agency have references? *(Have them sent to you. Follow-up on them.)*

Always personally check references on each caregiver. Keep in mind that your parent is extremely vulnerable in this type of situation, so it is better to err on the side of caution.

Questionnaire for Caregivers:

YES	NO	
☐	☐	Does the caregiver have references? *(Request the names and how to contact them.)*
☐	☐	Is the caregiver professionally trained? *(check any that apply)*

☐ CPR ☐ Certified Nursing Assistance
☐ First Aid ☐ Local Caregiver Training Program
☐ None ☐ Other_____

YES	NO	
☐	☐	Does the caregiver demonstrate good problem-solving skills?

Ask the caregiver questions, such as how he or she would handle a medical emergency and who they would call if unclear of how to meet your parent's need.

YES	NO	
☐	☐	Is the caregiver courteous to family? Your parent's friends? Your aging parent?
☐	☐	Is the caregiver even-tempered?
☐	☐	Is the caregiver assertive? Is the caregiver able to say "no" while maintaining your parent's dignity and self-determination when appropriate?
☐	☐	Is the caregiver free of contagious diseases? *Have report on TB done annually.*
☐	☐	Is the caregiver fingerprinted and on file with the local authorities?
☐	☐	Is the caregiver vaccinated for Covid or are they willing to be tested? (Personal preference)

Should Your Parent Move in with You?

Having your parent move into your home is an honorable decision but it may be riddled with complications between you and your spouse, children, work, friends, or other relatives. Even in the best of circumstances, combining living situations can be stressful for everyone involved. For example, living with your parent can bring up unresolved emotional conflicts.

If the commute to your parent's home to care for them is more than you can handle, inviting your parent to live with you might seem like the ideal solution. But before you start clearing out your parent's closets, read this section and answer the questions in the following questionnaires.

Some considerations when considering living with your parent:
- Your relationships will change because the dynamics of the environment will change.
- Your relationship with your spouse or significant other will definitely need to make new adjustments—are they willing to do so?
- Are you prepared to cope with any disruptions to your lifestyle that these changes may bring about? If so, how do you plan to manage any potential impacts on your marital and family relationships?
- How do you anticipate your relatives will respond to this potential move? What are their opinions on whether it is an appropriate decision, and how do you think they believe the logistics of executing the move should be worked out?
  - One major consideration when blending your family with your aging parent is the cost and how this may impact your parent's estate
  - Understand that whenever you introduce a change in your parent's living arrangement, there will be extra costs that should be considered.

Caring for your aging parent, whether it be in their home or yours, requires a robust support system that must be available and ready to accommodate your parent's needs, as well as yours and your family's.

There are two questionnaires that are designed to help you understand some of the fundamental issues when discussing whether it is feasible to blend your household with your parent's.

- One questionnaire is designed to help you start thinking about the realities of living with your parent.
- The other questionnaire is designed to help your parent start thinking about the realities of living with their child and/or family.

Once both of you have filled out your respective questionnaire, review and discuss your answers before moving in together. Moving your parent into your home can be very complicated. Avoid making this decision without the benefit of support from your family.

Questionnaire #18: For the Adult Child

Remember these questions are critical for you to be clear about what you are willing to do.

☑ **Check any questions for which the answer is "yes":**
- ☐ Are you close to your parent?
- ☐ Can you express anger to your parent without feeling guilty?
- ☐ Can you listen to your parent's feelings without becoming defensive?
- ☐ If your parent disapproves of something you say or do, can you still feel good about yourself?
- ☐ Can you treat your parent as an adult, not a child?
- ☐ Does your spouse like and get along with your parent?
- ☐ Does your parent like and get along with your spouse?
- ☐ If children are involved, do they get along with your parent?
- ☐ Does your parent get along with your children?

If you answered "yes" to all these questions, then living together may work.

If you did not answer "yes" to all these questions, you'll need to give this decision some serious, careful consideration.

Questionnaire #19: For the Parent

Remember these questions are critical for you to be clear about what you are willing to do.

☑ **Check any questions for which the answer is "yes":**
- ☐ Are you clear about your expectations in joining your child's household?
- ☐ Are you close to your child?
- ☐ Can you talk openly with your child about your feelings?
- ☐ Can you accept your child as an adult with needs and values that may differ from your own?
- ☐ Can you refrain from giving advice unless asked?
- ☐ Can you create your own entertainment and socialization experiences?
- ☐ Do you get along with your child's spouse?
- ☐ If no, can you prevent your feelings from interfering with your child's marriage?
- ☐ Do you get along with your grandchildren who may be living in the same household or who visit frequently?
- ☐ If no, can you prevent your feelings from interfering with your relationship with your child?

If you answered "yes" to all these questions, then living together may work.

If you did not answer "yes" to all these questions, you'll need to give this decision some serious, careful consideration.

If Your Parent Moves in With You

 Be careful not to sell your parent's home or give away the furniture *(or move your parent into a new community)* until you are sure living arrangements will work out. This is not to say living with a parent can't work. It can-as long as both of you know what the pitfalls are and have a plan for handling them.

Therefore, you must discuss the following issues before you make such a big move:

- What will your parent's role be in your combined household?
- What will yours be?
- How will you divide up the housework?
- What does somebody do when they want privacy or free time?
- How will you ensure that you and your spouse still have time together, and that the needs of any children still living at home are met?

You Need to Discuss Finances—
No matter how uncomfortable it may be to do so.

If moving in together is not an option but your parents can no longer live independently without support, you may need to investigate other living arrangement options.

Continued Care Retirement Communities

Senior living communities typically include independent living cottages/apartments, an assisted living facility, memory care units, and sometimes skilled nursing. Residents can transition between these levels of care as their needs change. Some CCRC communities allow the resident to age in place with private duty caregivers assisting them up to 12-hours daily.

- If the resident needs 24-hour care they may be required to move to the appropriate level of care in the facility.

- An exception is if the resident is in hospice. If this is the case, they can obtain private duty caregivers and will not be required to move from their apartment.
- It is always important to review the policies and regulations of the CCRC before you move your parent into one.
  - It is highly recommended that an attorney reviews the contract to be sure your parent's rights are intact and they can remain in the apartment without moving through the system if they can afford private duty caregivers.
  - Be sure to learn and understand what the exceptions are.

The drawback is that such communities tend to be expensive. Most require a substantial move-in fee as well as monthly maintenance payments. An important consideration is the refund policies for any upfront community or entrance fees. It's crucial to understand if, and when, those fees may be returned, and any conditions around length of residency.

Additionally, families should inquire about the community's visitor policies and protocols, especially in light of lessons learned during the COVID-19 pandemic. Your parent may be subject to restrictions, such as no visitors or isolation, if they become ill and the community is following public health guidelines. This can impact their quality of life and ability to receive support from their loved ones.

Remember:

Moving into a setting like this has wonderful opportunities and great support but it is a business and therefore your aging parent (and you) will be subjected to their rules and policies. This is a major difference in living arrangements since most people living in their own homes make the rules.

Your loved one needs to be involved in the selection process.

LeadingAge, an association of 6,000 not-for-profit organizations dedicated to improving senior living, recommends that prospective residents ask five questions when considering a continuing care retirement community.

Questions to Ask a CCRC Representative
1. What is included in the monthly fee?
2. What kind of emergency response systems do you have?
3. What is the difference between independent and assisted living, and when would they have to move to assisted living?
4. Can my parent remain in independent living when their needs change, and how is aging in place supported?
5. Can I review the residency agreement?

Action:
- Review the AARP website for more detailed information on CCRCs. This website can help guide you and your parent on what is important to know and understand before you select this option. *www.aarp.org/caregiving/basics/info-2017/continuing-care-retirement-communities.html*
- AARP offers a printer-ready worksheet allows you to write down information and assess plans for long-term care: *www.aarp.org/caregiving/basics/info-2017/continuing-care-retirement-communities.html*

Residential Care/Group Home or Assisted Living Facilities

There are two types of assisted living arrangements:

1) **Board and Care homes**, called residential care facilities or group homes, are small private facilities, with 20 or fewer residents.
    a. The rooms may be private or shared.
    b. Residents receive personal care and meals, and have staff available around the clock. Nursing and medical care usually are not provided on site.
    c. Many of these settings will allow a resident to have Hospice.

Questions to ask that will help you determine if this is the appropriate living arrangement for your aging parent:

- What is a typical day like for the residents?
- How does the staff help residents who have problems with incontinence, and are incontinence supplies provided under the residence fees or not?
- What safety precautions are in place for any residents with memory problems or a tendency to wander?
- Does the board and care home provide transportation to medical appointments or for shopping and entertainment?
- What opportunities are available for exercise?
- How frequently does the staff take vitals - blood pressure, pulse, temperature?
- Are weekly menus prepared? How are special dietary needs handled? Are snacks available between meals?
- May friends and relatives visit, and what kind of privacy do they have when they do?
- What emergency procedures are in place?

A good resource for more information about assessing Board & Care homes: *https://www.seniorly.com/board-and-care-home*

2) **Assisted Living Facilities** are for people who need help with daily care, but not as much help as a nursing home provides. They range in size from as few as 25 residents to 120 or more.

  a. Generally, 3 levels of care (supervisory, personal, or directed care) are offered, with residents paying more for higher levels of care.

  b. Assisted living residents usually live in their own apartments or rooms and share common areas.

  c. They have access to many services, including up to three meals a day; assistance with personal care; help with medications, housekeeping, and laundry; 24-hour supervision, security, and on-site staff; and social and recreational activities.

✍ **Note:** Exact arrangements vary from state to state. Be sure to check your state's regulations for assisted living facilities on the National Center for Assisted Living's website. https://www.ahcancal.org/Assisted-Living/Policy/Pages/state-regulations.aspx.

Tips to help you determine if this is the appropriate level of care:

- Arrange to be there during mealtimes or have lunch with residents, to give you a better sense of what it's like to live there.
- Ask questions about staff members, including their qualifications and whether they receive additional training from the facility.
- Visit multiple times and observe how employees interact with residents.
- Ask about the facility's suggestion, complaint and grievance procedures, and whether it has resident and family councils to provide feedback.
- Consider having a financial advisor and/or a lawyer review the agreement. If you need help locating one, contact the National Academy of Elder Law Attorneys at *www.naela.org*.

Use this website to get to your state's list of affiliated care facilities: *https://members.ahcancal.org/About-Us/Our-Affiliates*

☑ Checklist: Choosing an Assisted Living Facility

Knowing how to choose an assisted living facility is an important way to help your aging parent. The following is a list of questions to ask when considering an assisted living facility.

YES	NO	
☐	☐	Is this facility licensed by the state, county, or city?
☐	☐	Is the cost of services clearly stated?
☐	☐	Can my parent afford the cost of this facility?
☐	☐	Are the staff members trained to meet the needs of the residents?
☐	☐	Are there staff members on duty 24 hours per day?
☐	☐	Is the staff friendly?
☐	☐	Does the staff interact well with the residents?
☐	☐	Do the other residents appear happy?
☐	☐	Will my parent feel safe in this location?
☐	☐	Will the staff work with my parent's physician and home health staff when needed?
☐	☐	Does the facility have supervised activities?
☐	☐	Does the facility have a full-time activities director?
☐	☐	Does the facility have a full-time recreation person?
☐	☐	Are there activities in/from the community at large?
☐	☐	Is there a wellness program?
☐	☐	Are there laundry and housekeeping services?
☐	☐	Is there medication supervision?
☐	☐	Is there personal care service?
☐	☐	Is there transportation service to go shopping or to doctor appointments?
☐	☐	Are there barber/beauty shop services?
☐	☐	Do these services cost extra?
		Which ones and how much?_____

☐	☐	Are the rooms comfortable?
☐	☐	Can my parent bring his or her own furniture?
☐	☐	If not, are the furnishings provided comfortable?
☐	☐	Do the rooms have smoke detectors and sprinklers?
☐	☐	Can the residents call for help at night and receive prompt assistance?
☐	☐	Are there smoking regulations? What are they?
☐	☐	Are there grab bars and a seat in the shower?
☐	☐	Can my parent bring his or her own furniture?
☐	☐	How many bathrooms are available? Are there rooms with a private bathroom or must these facilities be shared?
☐	☐	Are three meals per day provided and is the quantity and quality adequate?
☐	☐	Are special dietary needs considered in meal preparation?
☐	☐	Is this location convenient for family and friends to visit?
☐	☐	Are the visiting hours convenient?
☐	☐	Is there an area where your parent may have private visits?
☐	☐	If your parent has a pet, are they allowed, and are there any size restrictions?

Shared Housing

This is a living arrangement in which two or more older persons share a home. Some are sponsored by community or church groups; many employ a full-time staff to help residents with shopping, cooking, and cleaning.

To find out more about this type of housing check with The National Shared Housing Resource Center. This is a network of independent non-profit home sharing programs across the United States. Their goals are to raise awareness of the benefits of home sharing, and to encourage best practices and cross learning among programs. You can find the list of programs for many states here: https://nationalsharedhousing.org/program- directory/

Skilled Nursing Facilities

Skilled nursing facilities, also commonly referred to as nursing homes, are for individuals with serious medical issues or dementia and who require 24/7 professional medical care.

People enter a nursing home for various reasons, such as recovering from an illness, injury, or surgery, managing chronic health conditions or disabilities that necessitate ongoing nursing support, or needing specialized care for dementia or Alzheimer's disease. These facilities provide round-the-clock medical attention and supervision that may be beyond the capabilities of a family to manage at home.

Evaluating whether a nursing home is the appropriate next step for your parent's care needs is an important consideration, but it should always be considered a last resort. The purpose of this option is to meet your parent's medical care needs. These are needs that may require specialized therapy and a professionally trained care staff that includes nurses, certified nursing assistants, rehabilitation staff, physical therapists, occupational therapists, and speech therapists.

If your parent's care needs require 24-hour support with a minimum of two staff members per shift to assist with basic ADL's (transferring, ambulating, bathing), or if your parent is bedridden and requires total care, then a nursing facility may be the best option.

"**Your Guide to Choosing a Nursing Home or Other Long-term Services & Support**" can help you make informed decisions about nursing home care, whether you're planning ahead or need to make an unexpected decision: https://www.medicare.gov/care-compare/en/assets/resources/nursing-home/02174-nursing-home-other-long-term-services.pdf.

This guide will explain how to find nursing homes or services, how care is paid for, what your parent's rights are as a nursing home resident, and what alternatives are available.

This pdf also contains a comprehensive nursing home evaluation checklist and data gathering tool.

Here is the process to help you find a nursing home for your aging parent:

- Ask friends, family, doctors, etc., if they have any experience or recommendations to share. Visit www.medicare.gov/care-compare for a provider list or utilize the Eldercare Locator at *https://eldercare.acl.gov/Public/Index.aspx.*
- Compare the quality of the nursing homes you're considering.
- Visit the nursing homes you're interested in or have someone visit for you.
- Choose the nursing home that best meets your family's needs.

Because not all types of facilities are available in every community, you may want to contact the local Area Agency on Aging to find out what is available in your parent's county. Call 1-800-677-1116.

6

Navigating Healthcare Insurance

IN THIS CHAPTER:

- **Medicare is Always Changing**
- **What Type of Insurance Does Your Parent Have?**
- **Original Medicare and Medicare Advantage Plans**
- **Some Key Terms Regarding Original Medicare**
- **Original Medicare Benefits Has Three Parts**
- **Medicare Advantage Plans**
- **Medicare: What You Need to Know**
- **Veterans Administration Healthcare Benefits**
- **Comparing Different Types of Medicare Advantage Plans**

Original Medicare, Medicare Advantage Plans, Medigap insurance, Medicaid, and Long-Term Care insurance are the main options for your parent's healthcare coverage.

The goal of this chapter is to help you find your way through these options to identify what is the best coverage available for your parent.

Medicare is Always Changing

It is important that you stay up-to-date on the decisions and discussions that Congress is making regarding Medicare issues.

For the most up-to-date information about Medicare programs and options, call the Medicare Information Line (Health Care Financing Administration). This is the federal agency that administers the Medicare Program. **Call 1-800-633-4227 or visit www.medicare.gov**.

All people with Medicare have rights and protections that are defined in the Medicare Bill of Rights. These are: *(Excerpt from "Medicare and You Handbook" 2022)*

- Be treated with courtesy, dignity, and respect at all times.
- Be protected from discrimination.
- Have personal and health information kept private.
- Get information in a way they understand from Medicare, healthcare providers, and, under certain circumstances, contractors.
- Learn about their treatment choices in clear language they can understand and participate in treatment decisions.
- Get Medicare information and health care services in a language they understand.
- Get Medicare information in an accessible format, like braille or large print.
- Get answers to their Medicare questions.
- Have access to doctors, specialists, and hospitals for medically necessary services.
- Get Medicare-covered services in an emergency.
- Get a decision about health care payment, coverage of items and services, or drug coverage. When your parent or their provider files a claim, they'll get a notice about what will and won't be covered. This notice comes from one of these:
  - Medicare
  - The Medicare Advantage Plan (Part C) or other Medicare Health Plan
  - The Medicare drug plan for Medicare drug coverage (Part D)
- If there is a disagreement with the decision of the claim, the patient has the right to file **an appeal**.

If you feel your parent's Medicare coverage was denied inappropriately, your parent can file an appeal online at:

www.medicare.gov/claims-appeals/how-do-i-file-an-appeal.

> **NOTE:**
>
> If you have concerns about the quality of care and other services your parent is receiving from a Medicare provider, they can file a complaint online at https://www.medicare.gov/claims-appeals/how-to-file-a-complaint-grievance.
>
> No matter which Medicare option your parent chooses, your parent has the right to challenge a denial of care or coverage through an appeal process.

If your parent is getting Medicare services from a hospital, skilled nursing facility, home health agency, comprehensive outpatient rehabilitation facility, or hospice, and you think your parent's Medicare-covered services are ending too soon (or that your parent is being discharged too soon), you can ask for a fast appeal (also known as an "immediate appeal" or an "expedited appeal"). **A fast appeal only covers the decision to end services.**

- If you are unavailable to help, your parent can appoint a representative to help.
- A representative can be a family member, friend, advocate, attorney, financial advisor, doctor, or anyone else who will act on behalf of your parent or you.
- For more information online, go to https://www.medicare.gov/claims-appeals/how-do-i-file-an-appeal.

You can also get help filing an appeal from your State Health Insurance Assistance Program (SHIP). Additionally, you may need to start a separate appeals process for any items or services your parent may have received after the decision to end services.

What Type of Insurance Does Your Parent Have?

Identify what type of health insurance your parent has since much of your parent's healthcare will be covered by some form of insurance. You need to understand what this insurance is: Tricare, VA Benefits, Federal employee health benefits/retirees, or Railroad Retirement Board.

Once the type is identified, call for more information about benefits:

- Medicare.gov/talk-to-someone or call 1-800-MEDICARE.
- Department of Defense Tricare—get information online at: **Tricare4u.com or call 866-773-0404.**
- Department of Veterans Affairs (VA)—get information online at: **www.VA.gov, or call 800-827-1000.**
- Office of Personnel Management—Federal Employee Health Benefits Program for retired federal employees. Get information online at:
  www.opm.gov/healthcare-insurance, or call 888-767-6738.
- Railroad Retirement Board (RRB)—If your parent qualifies for benefits, get information online at:
  www.rrb.gov, or call 877-772-5772.
- Indian Health Services (IHS)—
  Note: *Getting Medicare does not affect your ability to get services through the IHS and tribal health facilities.*
  Get information online at:
  https://www.ihs.gov/forpatients/faq/ To effectively care for your parent's needs, you must understand what options are available to increase the insurance coverage if needed.

Original Medicare and Medicare Advantage Plans

If you are satisfied with your parent's current Medicare coverage, you don't need to change or do anything.

As long as your parent has Medicare Parts A and B you can always switch to a different Medicare option during open enrollment.

- Open enrollment is between October to December of the current year to change options for the following year.
- If your parent has end-stage renal disease, their options will be limited.

Is your parent enrolling in Medicare for the first time?

By default, the government will automatically give them Original Medicare coverage unless your parent has selected another option.

If your parent is considering changing from one Medicare option to another, don't rely only on information provided by the various plans.

- Get additional information from HCFA. **Call 1-800-633-4227**.
- To sign up for a particular option *(other than Original Medicare)*, call the plan and ask for an enrollment form.
- If your parent enrolls in a Medicare option and gives up his or her Medigap or retiree health insurance, they may not be able to get the same coverage back later if they change their mind.

Before they change be sure to:

- Check with your parent's union or former employer plan.
- Check if there are any new laws limiting your parent's opportunity to get Medigap coverage.
- Call your parent's state health insurance assistance program to find out if there will be a problem.

If your parent wants to leave a Medicare Option Plan for Original Medicare coverage:

- Send a letter to the current plan asking to disenroll your parent.
- Original Medicare coverage will automatically begin on the first day of the month after the plan receives and accepts your letter.
- If you want Medigap insurance to accompany Original Medicare, ask your parent's state health insurance assistance program about Medigap options, or **call 800-633-4227**.

Some Key Terms Regarding Original Medicare

The Assignment is the rate that Medicare has determined is reasonable for a particular procedure.

- If a healthcare provider accepts "assignment," that provider agrees to accept these rates.
- Medicare pays 80% of the assignment rate.

Medicare approved services—Medicare will only cover medical expenses that fit their criteria for treatment.

- Always check to be sure the provider is working within the criteria of Medicare.
- If they are not and your parent accepts the treatment, your parent will have to pay for it.

Medigap (supplemental insurance)—This is insurance that pays for the 20% portion that Medicare does not pay.

- This 20% is based on the assignment only.
- It will also pay for hospital and medical expenses and deductibles.
- There are ten standard Medigap insurance programs that cover the basic copayments and deductibles. Several have additional coverage for expenses Medicare does not cover.
- For more information, contact the local **Medicare Information Line or call HCFA at 800-633-4227**. *Ask for information on Medigap insurance.*

Only the Original Medicare Coverage is Available Nationally

Original Medicare is a federally funded program to provide medical/hospital/hospice coverage to the elderly and the disabled.

With the Original Medicare program:

- Your parent can choose any physician, hospital, or medical services that are certified by Medicare.
- Your parent can also choose when to see a specialist, and which specialist to see.

Original Medicare Benefits Has Three Parts

1) Medicare Part A:

Your parent is automatically assigned as soon as they are eligible.
Medicare "Part A" is hospital insurance that covers:

- Hospitalization
- Skilled nursing facility care
- Home health care
- Hospice Care
- Blood transfusions

2) Medicare Part B:

Your parent is automatically enrolled unless your parent has refused.

- If your parent accepts Part B, a monthly premium will automatically be deducted from your parent's Social Security check.
- Medicare Part B is medical insurance that covers:
  Medical expenses *(including physicians and many of the medical services not covered by Part A)*

3) Original Medicare Expanded Benefits:

Reminder: check with the most current *"Medicare and You"* handbook for up-to-date covered benefits.

Disadvantages of Original Medicare

- The out-of-pocket expenses.
- No prescription drug coverage—must get a separate drug policy.
- Your parent will need to purchase Medigap insurance, which can be costly.

Medicare Advantage Plans

Medicare Advantage Plans, sometimes called "Part C" or "MA Plans", are offered by Medicare-approved private companies that must follow rules set by Medicare.

Most Medicare Advantage Plans include drug coverage (Part D).

If your parent has a Medicare Advantage Plan, your parent still has Medicare but will get most of their Part A and Part B coverage from the Medicare Advantage Plan, not the Original Medicare.

- Medicare Advantage Plans provide all of Part A and Part B benefits, excluding clinical trials, hospice services, and, for a temporary time, some new benefits that come from legislation or national coverage determinations.
- If your parent has a Medicare Advantage Plan, Original Medicare will still help cover the cost of hospice care, some new Medicare benefits, and some costs for clinical research studies.
- All Medicare Advantage Plans must cover all emergency and urgent care, and almost all of the medically necessary services *Original Medicare* covers.
- Some plans can also choose to cover even more benefits, such as over-the-counter drugs, services like transportation to doctor visits, and services that promote health and wellness.
- Plans can also tailor their benefit packages to offer additional benefits to certain chronically ill enrollees.
- In most cases, your parent might need to use healthcare providers who participate in the plan's network.

Remember:

Your parent must use the card from their Medicare Advantage Plan to get their Medicare-covered services.

Caution:

Be sure your parent keeps their red, white, and blue Medicare card in a safe place because they need it if your parent wants to switch back to Original Medicare.

Companies offering Medicare Advantage Plans must follow rules set by Medicare, however:

- Each Medicare Advantage Plan can charge different out-of-pocket costs and have different rules for how to get services.
  <u>For example</u>: *If a referral is necessary to see a specialist if you have to go to doctors, facilities, or suppliers that belong to the plan's network for non-emergency or non-urgent care.*
- Providers can join or leave a plan's provider network any time during the year. Your parent's plan can also change the providers in the network any time during the year.
  - If this happens, your parent usually won't be able to change plans but can choose a new provider until the enrollment period in October-December.
  - The plan will make a good faith effort to give at least 30 days' notice that your parent's provider is leaving the plan so there is time to choose a new provider.
- These rules can change each year so be sure to keep informed.
- The plan must notify you about any changes before the start of the next enrollment year.

Remember:

Your parent has the option each year to keep their current plan, choose a different plan, or switch to Original Medicare (during the enrollment period from October-December).

Comparing Different Types of Medicare Advantage Plans

Here are brief descriptions of the other Medicare options currently available. Remember that these plans may not yet be available in your parent's area.

1) **Preferred Provider Organization (PPO) Plan:**
   This is like an HMO but enrollees can go outside the plan for services.
   - The enrollee agrees to share the cost of care outside the plan's network of providers.
   - Usually, your parent will not have to pick a primary care physician; in other words, they can go to any physician affiliated with the plan.
     - Advantage: Out-of-pocket expenses are lower than in the Original Medicare program.
     - Disadvantage: Higher out-of-pocket expenses than in a traditional HMO plan.

2) **HMO Point-of-Service (HMOPOS) Plan:**
   This HMO plan may allow your parent to get some services out of network for a higher copayment or coinsurance.
   - This is like an HMO but these plans are more often found in rural areas.
   - All routine care must come from within the POS network.
   - Usually, these plans are managed by the physicians and hospitals.

Advantage: Out-of-pocket expenses are lower than in the Original Medicare program.

Disadvantage: There may be a limited number of providers in any given area.

3) Medical Savings Account (MSA) Plan:

This plan deposits money into a special account which varies by plan.

- MSA plans do not charge a premium, but your parent must continue to pay their Part B premium.
- For more information **visit Medicare.gov**.

4) Private Fee-for-Service (PFFS) Plan:

This plan will determine how much your parent pays for services. Some contract with a network of providers. *Check with the specific plan for more information.*

5) Special Needs Plan (SNP):

This plan provides benefits and services to people with specific diseases, certain healthcare needs, or limited incomes.

Go online to **Medicare.gov/plan-compare** to find and compare Medicare Advantage Plans to see if SNP plans are available in the area.

Resources for More Information

- Order the *"Medicare and You"* handbook by calling **800-633-4227**, or download the PDF online at **https://www.medicare.gov/publications**
- Contact your state health insurance assistance program. Their number is listed in the back of the Medicare handbook.
- Visit the Medicare website at **www.medicare.gov**.
- Contact AARP (**www.aarp.org**) to request one of the following pamphlets:
  - *"Nine Ways to Get the Most from Your Medicare"*
  - Managed Care Plan *"Medicare Basics"*
- *"Choosing the Right Medigap Plan"* **https://www.aarp.org/health/medicare-insurance/info-2023/guide-to-medigap-plans.html**
- *"Medicare Rights and Responsibilities"* (these are also listed in this chapter) **https://www.aarp.org/health/medicare-qa-tool/basic-medicare-rights-and-protections/**

Medicaid: What You Need to Know

Medicaid is a public entitlement program. That means Medicaid benefits are available only to those individuals whose income is at or below the specified income level, and those who qualify as needing additional support.

- There are established criteria for both financial and medical needs to be eligible for Medicaid benefits.
- Long-term care benefits are available through Medicaid for those who qualify.

A second program covered through Medicaid is the Qualified Medicare Beneficiary (QMB) benefit.

- QMB provides financial assistance by returning (not deducting) the Medicare premium from the recipient's social security check and by paying all co-pays to physicians, outpatient clinics, and hospitals.
- The recipient is still fully covered by Medicare.

A third program covered through Medicaid is the Specified Low Income Medicare Beneficiary (SLMB).

SLMB provides financial assistance by returning *(not deducting)* the Medicare premium from the recipient's social security check. However, it does not pick up any co-pays. The recipient is still fully covered by Medicare.

How does your parent qualify for Medicaid? Many criteria are considered in each situation. Basically, your parent must have a medical need and be at (or below) the specified income level.

You can call your local Area Agency on Aging and request the phone number for the nearest Medicaid office, or you can call the **Medicare Information Line at 800-633-4227** to request information about Medicaid, or online at:
https://www.medicaid.gov/about-us/contact-us/index.html.

Don't overlook a benefit your parent may be entitled to receive. Call the Medicaid office to obtain the criteria for qualifying for benefits.

Veterans Administration Healthcare Benefits: What You Need to Know

If your parent served in the Armed Services with an honorable discharge, they might qualify for some Veterans Administration benefits. Call the Department of Veterans Affairs in your state to inquire about services and eligibility.

Some healthcare benefits a veteran might be eligible for are:
- Veterans Administration hospital
- Nursing home care
- Home health services
- Outpatient treatment
- Medical exams
- Related medical services during rehabilitation
- Consultation
- Counseling
- Alcohol and drug dependence treatment

Caution:

If your parent is placed on observation status in the hospital, ensure that their status is changed to "Admitted" if they need to stay in the hospital for longer than 48 hours.

Failure to do this may cause the need for your parent to pay for the extra expense of the days beyond what is considered Observational Status. When in doubt, be sure to discuss this with the case manager in the hospital.

7

Navigating Long-Term Care Insurance

IN THIS CHAPTER:

- **Long-Term Care Insurance: What You Need to Know**
- **What Kinds of Policies Can Your Parent Buy?**
- **Questions About Long-Term Care Insurance Policy**
- **Checklist: Information about your Parent's Long-Term Care Insurance Policy**
- **When Shopping for Long-Term Care Insurance - How to Assess What your Parent is Buying**

There are two important questions to ask when beginning to care for your aging parent:

1) What if your aging parent needs care beyond what you can offer? Often someone in the family will bear most of the caregiving duties. This can put a significant strain on the caregiver's own relationships and self-care, as they may neglect their own needs to meet the demands of caring for their parent. Have a backup plan or additional support ready for these types of instances.

2) Who pays for the care of your aging parent if you cannot provide the care alone with family and friends? First, government programs may be able to provide financial assistance if your parent meets the eligibility requirements. Alternatively, if your parent has personal financial resources, they may be able to directly cover the cost of caregivers. Another solution is long-term care insurance. This specialized type of insurance policy can reimburse

policyholders for some or all of the costs associated with long-term care services. Purchasing a long-term care policy in advance can help prepare for these future needs.

The purpose of long-term care planning is to help your aging parent compensate for limitations in his or her ability to function independently. The information in this section will help you understand the needs and options of long-term care insurance.

The value of Long-Term care insurance policies should also be considered by the family of the aging parent as soon as possible. Children between 40-50 seem to be in the best age group to purchase their own Long-Term care Insurance. They will be less likely to have higher premiums and can possibly have their LTC insurance paid up by retirement.

If your parent has a major illness or injury, such as a stroke, heart attack, or broken hip, and needs assistance with daily living activities (bathing or dressing), they may need long-term care. In some cases, they may only require short-term nursing home care or in-home assistance for a limited period. However, in other situations, they may need these long-term care services for many months, years, or even for the remainder of their life. It's hard to know if and when they'll need long-term care, but the following statistics may help.

- Life expectancy after age 65 is about 19.4 years (20.6 years for females and 18 years for males).
- The longer people live, the greater the chance they'll need help due to chronic conditions.
- About 70% of people who reach age 65 are expected to need some form of long-term care at least once in their lifetime.
- About 35% of people who reach age 65 are expected to enter a nursing home at least once in their lifetime.
- Of those who are in a nursing home, the average stay is one year.

- From 2015 to 2055, the number of people aged 85 and older will almost triple, from more than 6 million to more than 18 million.
- This growth is certain to lead to an increase in the number of people who need long-term care.

Long-Term Care Insurance was introduced in the 1980s as nursing home insurance but now often covers services in other facilities. It is essential that you thoroughly review and understand the details of the policy. This will ensure you know exactly what services your parent's long-term care insurance will and will not pay for as their care requirements evolve over time.

Policies may cover the following: *(Remember not all policies are the same so review carefully what your parent's LTC insurance will cover)*

- Nursing home care
- Home care
- Respite care
- Hospice care
- Personal care in your home
- Services in assisted living facilities
- Services in adult day care centers

Long-Term Care Insurance: What You Need to Know

If your aging parent has custodial care needs only, Medicare will not cover the cost even if it is necessary to place your parent in a nursing home.

- Custodial care is provided by non-medical personnel to assist with activities of daily living.
- Medicare does not cover this level of services.
- This assistance is generally an out-of-pocket expense.

> **FACT:**
>
> Medicare and Medicaid have their own definition of skilled care and custodial care. Refer to your parent's Medicare Handbook for this information. To obtain this handbook, call the **Medicare Information Line at 1-800-633-4227**, or see the PDF online at: **www.medicare.gov/Pubs/pdf/10050-medicare-and-you.pdf**.

- Medicare and Medigap insurance does not pay for:
    - Long-term care homemaker services
    - Custodial care services for long-term care
- Medicaid does pay for nursing home care and community home-based services for long-term care needs, provided your parent meets the federal poverty guidelines for income and assets and the criteria for medical eligibility

> **✎ NOTE:**
>
> State laws differ about how much money and assets your parent is allowed to have and keep.

Contact your parent's state Medicaid office, Area Agency on Aging, Department of Social Services, or the local Social Security office to learn about the rules in your parent's state, as state laws governing the providers of long-term care and the terms used to describe these providers vary widely.

Here is a list of some of the long-term care providers you may encounter as you begin to evaluate your parent's need for long-term care:

- Nursing homes
- Assisted living facilities
- Adult day-care program
- Home-care agencies
- Day/temporary help agencies
- Board and care homes
- Adult care homes

What Kinds of Policies Can Your Parent Buy?

First, a caution: Long-term care insurance policies are not standardized like the Medigap supplemental insurance.

Below is a list of the different types of long-term care insurance policies available:

1. Individual policies: Most long-term care policies are sold to individuals.
2. Policies through your employer: Check to see if your parent's retirement plan through their employer has included a Long-term Care policy.
3. Association policies: In most states, association policies must allow members to keep their coverage after they leave the association.
4. Life insurance policies: Some life insurance companies offer access to the life insurance death benefit and cash value under certain specified conditions before death, such as terminal illness, permanent confinement in a nursing home, or long-term care. This is often referred to as an "accelerated benefit" provision.
5. Partnership programs: Some states have programs designed to assist persons with the financial consequences of spending down to Medicaid eligibility standards. Check with your parent's state insurance department to see if a partnership program is available there.

Questions to Ask About Your Parent's Long-Term Care Insurance Policy

If your parent has a long-term care policy or is purchasing a policy, it is critical that you understand the coverage for the variety of long-term services available. Here is a list of questions to ask an agent about the long-term care insurance policy:

-   How are benefits paid?
-   Where is service covered?
-   What is not covered?

- How much coverage will your parent have?
  - What is the lifetime maximum?
  - What is the daily/monthly benefit amount?
- When is your parent eligible for benefits?
- When do benefits begin?
  - What is the elimination period?
  - What happens if your parent has a repeat need for this benefit?
- What happens when long-term care costs rise?
- Is there any inflation protection?
- Are there any other optional policy provisions available?
  - Third-party notification?
  - Waiver of premium?
  - Restoration of benefits?
  - Nonforfeiture benefits?
  - Premium refund upon death?

☑ Checklist: Information about your Parent's Long-Term Care Insurance Policy

Instructions:

Review your parent's long-term care insurance policy and check the boxes that identify the key points of this policy.

Be sure to ask questions about any benefits. Either your parent's insurance agent or the insurance company should be able to clarify this policy.

Name of company_____

Address _____

City _____State_____ Zip Code_____

Phone _____Fax_____

Email _____

Website _____

Important phone numbers:

Agent's name_____

Phone _____ Fax_____

Email _____

Claims representative_____

Phone _____ Fax_____

Toll-free # _____

Address to send claims _____

City _____State_____ Zip Code_____

Phone _____ Fax_____

Toll-free _____

Total amount of premium *(include all riders and discounts)*: $ _____
Type of reimbursement:
- ☐ Expense incurred
- ☐ Indemnity

What levels of care are covered by this policy? Check all that are applicable:
- ☐ Nursing care: Must have skilled personnel or special medical treatment
- ☐ Personal care: bathing, dressing, eating, continence, toileting, transferring
- ☐ Home health care: must have care by a therapist or registered RN
- ☐ Other

Where can this level of care be offered? Check all that apply:
- ☐ Nursing home
- ☐ Home
- ☐ Assisted living facility
- ☐ Adult day care
- ☐ Other

What is the Maximum Daily Benefit?

Maximum daily amount: $ _____

Maximum per hour: $ _____

Maximum number of hours per day: _____

What are the limits on the number of days per year?
Maximum number of days:

Per week: _____ Per month: _____ Per year: _____

What is the length of benefit period for the levels of care?

Nursing care: _____

Personal care: _____

Nursing home:_____

Home care: _____

Adult day care:_____

Assisted living facility:_____

Other: _____

How long before the benefits begin for each level of care (elimination or
waiting period)? How many days?

Nursing care: _____

Personal care: _____

Nursing home:_____

Home care: _____

Adult day care:_____

Assisted living facility:_____

Other: _____

What are the benefit triggers used to determine eligibility for this policy?
(May need more than one, check all that apply)
☐ Physician certification of medical necessity
☐ Failure to perform activities of daily living
☐ Prior hospital confinement: How long? _____
☐ Cognitive impairment
☐ Other

Does this policy define clearly what activities of daily living needs are?

☐ Yes ☐ No

There are generally six: how many are required before eligibility occurs?

Check which ones:

☐ Bathing
☐ Toileting
☐ Dressing
☐ Continence
☐ Eating
☐ Transferring
☐ Other

Does this policy have separate benefit triggers for cognitive impairments?

☐ Yes ☐ No

What are they? _____

_____

Can you buy additional increments of coverage?

☐ Yes ☐ No

When? _____

How much? _____

Are benefits automatically increased to cover inflation?

☐ No

☐ Yes. What type of increase? _____

☐ Simple ☐ Compounded

When and how does this increase start? _____

_____

_____

Does your parent need to be receiving services before this starts?

☐ No ☐ Yes. How long?_____

Is there a nonforfeiture benefit?

☐ No

☐ Yes. What kind?_____

Does this policy have a return of premium benefit?

☐ Yes   ☐ No

Does this policy have a death benefit?

☐ Yes   ☐ No

What are the restrictions (if any) before this benefit is paid?

_____

_____

_____

Any additional information:

_____

_____

When Shopping for Long-Term Care Insurance – How to Assess What Your Parent is Buying?

Another word of caution: If your parent does not already have LTC insurance they may not be eligible due to their existing medical/mental problem. Health history is a factor in being a candidate for LTC insurance. The older your parent is the more costly the premium will be.

- Be sure you understand the policy, what it covers, and what it does not cover.
- Never pay cash for a long-term care policy.
- Always get the name, address, and telephone numbers of the agent and the company from whom they plan to purchase their long-term care insurance policy. Be sure you have a local or toll-free number.
- Check on the financial stability of the company they are considering.

Ratings are available at the following agencies listed below:

- A.M. Best Company **(800) 424-2378, https://web.ambest.com**
- Fitch Investors Service, Inc. **(212) 908-0500, www.fitchratings.com**
- Be sure to review your policy during the free-look period.
- It may be a good idea to have premiums automatically deducted from your parent's bank account.

[This chapter is based on literature developed by the National Association of Insurance Commissioners (NAIC). If you would like a more detailed information of long-term care insurance, the website at (https://content.naic.org/consumer/long-term-care-insurance.htm) is very comprehensive.]

The Definitive Guide to Providing Effective, Loving Care for Your Aging Parent

8

Loss, Grief, Terminal Illness & Death

IN THIS CHAPTER:

- **Real Story of Mary and Brenda**
- **Loss and Grief**
- **Questionnaire: Assessing Losses in Your Parent's Life**
- **Questionnaire: Recognizing General Characteristics of Grief**
- **Questionnaire: Recognizing Feelings Associated with Grief**
- **Questionnaire: Recognizing Behaviors Associated with Grief**
- **When Grief is Complicated**
- **Professional Grief Counseling**
- **Self-Help Groups**
- **Options for Care of the Terminally Ill**
- **Questionnaire: Questions About Curative Care**
- **Comfort Care**
- **When Death Occurs**
- **Checklist: What to do When Death Occurs**
- **Questionnaire: Funeral Service Instructions**
- **Questionnaire: Memorial Information**
- **Questionnaire: Obituary Information**

Story of Mary and Brenda:

Mary is the 87-year-old mother of Brenda. I had been assisting Brenda in coordinating care to her mother for several years. Recently Mary was diagnosed with Pancreatic Cancer and understood that this was a terminal illness. After discussing this with her family and friends she was clear that she did not want to take any treatments designed to cure this illness. However, her daughter Brenda, who was her mother's caregiver did not want her mother to give up.

Clearly, both had a sense of the pending death with different expectations:

Mary did not want to suffer or prolong her life with treatments that would create discomfort and Brenda wanted her mother to fight and do everything possible to stay alive. Brenda had worked very diligently to keep her mother happy, and met all her health, personal care needs, and was willing to continue through all the results of radiation, chemotherapy, and special diets.

Barbara, the geriatric care manager, met with Mary and Brenda to help them express their feelings openly and honestly with each other.

Brenda did not want to lose her mother, and Mary did not want to prolong her suffering. It was then Brenda realized that letting Mary have full authority over her future was not a failure of her role (and love) as a daughter and caregiver.

Barbara discussed the options for care, and both were ready to discuss Hospice care with Mary's doctor. Barbara contacted Hospice and requested they come to Mary's home to discuss how they would assist in keeping Mary comfortable and Brenda supported through this period of bereavement.

If your aging parent is diagnosed with a terminal illness, you will be dealing with one of the hardest tasks an adult child faces, experiencing the sad realization that your parent is very ill. This is a great loss of a very special relationship, one that holds a variety of meanings, experiences, and emotions. Additionally, the emotional trauma of watching your parent decline can create a need for compassionate support for yourself as well.

A very important part of providing support and care to your parents is to recognize your own beliefs, feelings, fears, and attitudes about death. Trying to provide care while grieving is a very complicated task, one fraught with love, anger, frustration, sadness, and guilt. These feelings are normal and only human.

So far, throughout this book you have been learning about how to care for your aging parent, to assure their care is being met to the best of your ability. However, it is also important to understand what your parent's beliefs, feelings, fears, and attitudes are about death, and to know what your parent's care options are.

In this chapter, you will learn to recognize when your parent is dealing with grief and loss, and how to best support that. You will find information and questionnaires designed to help you and your parent with this process. We will also discuss the different options for care and treatment to better cope with this experience. These include:

1) Overview of loss and grief, and several questionnaires to assist you in identifying how your parent may be responding to loss and grief.
   - Questionnaire: Assessing losses in your Parent's Life
   - Questionnaire: Recognizing General Characteristics of Grief
   - Questionnaire: Recognizing Behaviors Associated with Grief
   - Questionnaire: Recognizing Feelings Associated with Grief
2) What you need to know when grief is complicated.
3) Resources to help your aging parent cope with their loss and grief:
   - Professional Grief Counseling
   - Self-Help Groups
4) The three types of care when your parent has been diagnosed with a terminal illness.
   - Comfort care
   - Palliative care
   - Hospice care

5) What to do when your aging parent dies.
  - Checklist: What to do when a death occurs
    - Questionnaire: Questions to Ask Your Parent's Doctor about Curative Care
    - Questionnaire: Funeral Service Instructions
    - Questionnaire: Memorial Service
    - Questionnaire: Obituary information
    - Persons to be notified

Loss and Grief

To be an effective support to your aging parent there are some terms that you need to understand.

Grief is what you experience when you have suffered a loss. "Loss" is the key word here because grief not only applies to the way you feel after the death of a loved one, but also to the way one feels with the loss of something valuable. In looking at and understanding grief in a broader sense, you may be grieving for something almost your entire lifetime (a divorce or breakup, losing a job, or experiencing the loss of physical possessions through theft, fire, etc.) Understandably, the grief one experiences over many losses will differ in intensity and longevity.[1]

If your parent should receive a diagnosis of a major or terminal illness, there will be a series of powerful emotions that can absorb and deplete both your parent and you. It can produce intense emotional and physical pain. When someone's life has been shattered, they may confront a sense of panic in grappling with the numerous practical tasks and new realities they now face.

Grief is a high stressor, and it would be normal for your parent to have good and bad days. Stress negatively affects our immune system, with common complaints including colds, lingering flu, back and neck pain,

---

[1] https://childhoodbraintumor.org/grief-101-some-common-facts-and-characteristics-of-grief/

headaches, stomach upset, dizziness, insomnia, and new flare-ups of pre-existing illnesses.[2]

- Strong feelings of grief return on holidays, birthdays, anniversaries – and especially the yearly anniversary of the loss. This is normal and usually, the anticipation of these days is worse than the actual day. Your parent could let those around them know that such a date is approaching and ask for their understanding and support.[3]
- Grief takes a long time. It will take as long as it takes, and you need to have patience with your parent, as this is as new to them as it is to you.

Complicated Grief is when the grief process is unusual and exaggerated in a way that is unhealthy.

Loss is a common experience for people of all ages. It is important to understand that loss through death is one of many kinds of loss your parent can suffer. The grief resulting from death is usually the ultimate loss; however, it is not the only event that initiates catastrophic change.

Each loss that your parent experiences has emotional consequences. If you can identify the losses your parent has experienced, you will be better able to understand the feelings and behavior of your parent.

Examples of losses:

- Loss of physical function, independence, and control
- Loss of intellectual functioning
- Loss of work (retirement)
- Loss of good health and youth
- Loss of familiar surroundings or possessions
- Loss of relationships (divorce, breakups, empty nest, distancing)
- Loss through death
- Loss of purpose, or the shattering of a life-long dream

---

[2] https://childhoodbraintumor.org/grief-101-some-common-facts-and-characteristics-of-grief/

[3] https://childhoodbraintumor.org/grief-101-some-common-facts-and-characteristics-of-grief/

Questionnaire #20: Assessing Losses in Your Parent's Life

This questionnaire will help you focus on some of these potential losses. Place a check in the box for each loss your parent has experienced during the last year.

Has your parent recently lost a:

☐ Spouse   ☐ Significant other
☐ Close friend   ☐ Adult child
☐ Grandchild   ☐ Brother or sister
☐ Significant pet   ☐ Another person not mentioned

Has your parent lost most or all of his or her own birth family?
☐ Yes   ☐ No

Has your parent recently experienced physical losses such as:

☐ Eyesight   ☐ Hearing   ☐ Mobility   ☐ Speech
☐ Smell/taste   ☐ A limb   ☐ Health

Has your parent recently moved from familiar surroundings?
☐ Yes   ☐ No

Has your parent recently stopped working, either full-time, part-time, or as a volunteer?   ☐ Yes   ☐ No

Has your parent recently been diagnosed with a terminal or chronic disease?   ☐ Yes   ☐ No

Are there any other losses your parent has experienced over the past year?
☐ Yes   ☐ No

Action:

Write down a list of all the recent losses your aging parent is experiencing.

1. _____
2. _____
3. _____
4. _____
5. _____

The next three questionnaires are designed to help you focus on what specific grief symptoms your parent may be dealing with.

Questionnaire #21: Recognizing General Characteristics of Grief

☑ Check any statement or question that is true of your parent's current bodily sensations or exhibited behavior:

- ☐ Feeling new or more intense bodily distress
- ☐ Hollowness in the stomach
- ☐ Tightness in the chest or throat
- ☐ Oversensitivity to noise
- ☐ Breathlessness
- ☐ Weakness in muscles
- ☐ Lack of energy
- ☐ Dry mouth
- ☐ Disorganization
- ☐ Inability to concentrate or retain information
- ☐ Lack of interest or motivation
- ☐ Lowered tolerance level

Has your parent become preoccupied with images and focused memories of a loss?　☐ Yes　☐ No

Has your parent expressed guilt about what he/she might or might not have done to prevent the loss?　☐ Yes　☐ No

Has your parent expressed some unusual or uncharacteristic anger or hostility toward you or others?　☐ Yes　☐ No

Has there been an observable change in your parent's ability to take care of themself and do the things they've always done before?　☐ Yes　☐ No

Questionnaire #22: Recognizing Feelings Associated with Grief

☑ Check any statement that is true of your parent's current feelings. This will help you become familiar with their feelings associated with grief. It may help you be patient with the changes your parent may be experiencing.

- ☐ Sadness: this doesn't mean just crying
- ☐ Anger
- ☐ Guilt and self-reproach
- ☐ Anxiety
- ☐ Loneliness
- ☐ Fatigue
- ☐ Helplessness
- ☐ Yearning: wishing for what was lost
- ☐ Relief: often accompanied by guilt
- ☐ Numbness: lack of feeling

Questionnaire #23: Recognizing Behaviors Associated with Grief

☑ Check any statement that is true of your parent's current behavior. This will help you become familiar with their behaviors associated with grief. It may help you be patient with the changes your parent may be experiencing.

- ☐ Sleep disturbances
  - In adaptive (normal) grief this will correct itself
- ☐ Absent-minded behavior
  - Forgetfulness
  - Misplacing things
- ☐ Social withdrawal
  - Hard to connect with familiar people in familiar situations
- ☐ Dreams
  - Can be both pleasant and distressing dreams
- ☐ Avoiding reminders
  - Associated with social withdrawal
  - Also avoids things or places that trigger memories
- ☐ Searching and calling out
- ☐ Sighing
  - Feeling of breathlessness
- ☐ Restless overactivity
  - Feels a need to be moving constantly
- ☐ Crying
  - Relieves emotional distress
- ☐ Carrying objects that are reminders
  - Opposite of avoiding
  - Treasures belongings that are representative of loss

✍ **NOTES:**

Review each of these three questionnaires. Write down any signs or symptoms that are currently how your parent is behaving. These signs and symptoms are most likely normal. It is important for you to observe and understand how your parent may be feeling so that you can better help them through this grief and loss.

Also note that even though you have not been diagnosed with a terminal illness, you are reacting to this diagnosis. Be kind to yourself and reach out for help to get through this time.

When Grief is Complicated

If the feelings and behaviors you have just identified are exaggerated in intensity or your parent has not experienced any relief from grief over an extended period, your parent may be suffering from complicated grief. The following identifies four types of complicated grief.

- **Exaggerated grief reaction**

  This reaction is an intensified normal grief reaction, however, your aging parent is overwhelmed by these feelings and cannot cope. If this grief is left unaddressed, your parent may become clinically depressed or display other emotional problems.

- **Delayed grief reaction**

  This reaction is sometimes called inhibited, suppressed, or postponed grief reaction. Your parent may have had some reaction to the loss, but he or she closed off this reaction too soon.
  The problem is that when another loss occurs, the delayed grief will surface again. This can cause your parent significant suffering, and he or she may need professional help to sort it all out.

- **Chronic grief reaction**

  In this type of grief, your parent's reaction to his or her grief is excessive and has no resolution. This reaction lasts for many years and causes your parent to feel unfinished, which may create deeper emotional problems. Your parent will need professional help to recover from this grief.

- **Masked grief reaction**

  In this reaction, the person denies experiencing grief but experiences symptoms and behaviors associated with grief.
  The person does not see these symptoms as related to the loss. Symptoms can be physical, emotional, or mental.

When Your Parent Needs Professional Grief Counseling

When your parent's feelings and behaviors associated with grief are any of the following, professional help is needed:

1) They are lasting beyond what seems reasonable. (*Chronic grief reaction*)
2) They are so intense that they interfere with your parent's daily functioning. (*Exaggerated grief reaction*)
3) They do not seem to exist although you know the loss is profound. (*Delayed grief reaction*)
4) Your parent does not acknowledge that the feelings and behaviors are related to the known loss. (*Masked grief reaction*)

A professional therapist or counselor can be a psychologist, psychiatrist, social worker, or someone who has a master's degree in counseling, but they should have special training in grief counseling.

- The goal of grief therapy is to help your parent face, explore, and resolve the conflicts that occur around the loss...
- and to help your parent complete the process of grieving.
- This can be a painful and emotional process that will necessitate your support and understanding.
- The counselor may also want to talk with you about how you can provide support through this therapy.

> ✍ **NOTE:**
> If you recognize any of these four types of complicated grief in your parent, you will need to encourage him or her to seek professional help from a therapist trained in grief counseling.

> ✍ **NOTE:**
> You can locate a professional grief counselor by calling a local mental health clinic or a family service agency. If there are none of these in your community, perhaps a local funeral home would have a referral list of grief counselors.

Self-Help Groups

When the feelings and behaviors associated with grief are not exaggerated, delayed, chronic, or masked, you may want to encourage your parent to join a self-help support group that focuses on his or her particular loss. The "Caregiver Resources" chapter has a phone number for the Area Agency on Aging. They would be able to provide you with a list of local support groups.

Self-help groups have the following characteristics:
1) They are small, face-to-face interactive units.
2) They are composed of people who share a common situation, symptom, or experience.
3) They are self-governing.
4) They have no trained professional leader.
5) There is usually no charge to attend.

Self-help groups have three basic expectations:
1) Those joining have a strong need for help.
2) Members must be willing to share personal stories and feelings.
3) Members must have a common problem or need consistent with the focus of the group.

Self-help groups have several benefits:
1) They generate a sense of belonging.
2) They provide motivation to remain in the group and to continue to work with the group.
3) They offer acceptance that supports the expression of one's own emotions.
4) They provide a wide variety of information about how others have experienced and behaved and learned through their situations.

Diagnosed with a Terminal Illness: Options for Care for the Terminally Ill

If your parent has been diagnosed with a terminal illness, there are variable levels of care options available, and new terminology to become familiar with.

If your aging parent experiences a medical problem that's not related to the terminal illness, Medicare will cover curative care for that issue, although there may be some charges depending on your insurance.

Curative or Therapeutic Care—The issue of curative care comes up when a patient has a terminal illness and is considering hospice care. Curative or therapeutic care refers to treatments and therapies provided to a patient with the goal of curing an illness or condition.

- Examples: Antibiotics for bacterial infections, chemotherapy or radiation therapy for cancer, a cast for a broken bone, dialysis treatment for kidney failure, surgery for appendicitis, and acupuncture or dietary programs for certain conditions.
- Curative care can also include treatments that delay disease progression even when a cure is not possible.
- There are risks and benefits of any curative or therapeutic care therefore it is important to know what these are so you can make the best choices for your aging parent.
- The best way to learn about your parent's choices is from their parent's doctors and specialists.

In many situations, there is no single "right" healthcare decision because choices about treatment, medical tests, and health issues come with pros and cons.

Questionnaire #24: Questions to Ask Your Parent's Doctor about Curative Care

It is always good to write down anything you want to discuss with your parent's physician and to take notes when you are there. Be sure to ask for an explanation of anything you do not understand.

- ☐ Does my parent really need this test, treatment, or procedure?
- ☐ What do you expect the benefits to be?
- ☐ What are the risks?
- ☐ Are there simpler, safer options?
- ☐ What happens if my parent doesn't do anything?
- ☐ How much will it cost?
- ☐ How will it affect the quality of my parent's life and his/her ability to do the things they like to do?

Comfort Care

The term "comfort care" is used between doctors, and doctors and family, and refers to end-of-life care focused on providing relief and quality of life, rather than curative treatment. When doctors are talking to patients about reducing their care from life-prolonging or curative therapies, they discuss this approach as comfort-focused therapies.

Even though comfort care still involves medical therapy, the goals of the therapy are different. Comfort care often implies that the person is reducing the intensity of medical care because the burden outweighs the benefits. It also generally means the individual recognizes that they are nearing the end of their life.

Broaching the Topic of Comfort Care with Your Parent's Doctor

Doctors, or anyone, can rarely forecast exactly how long someone will live, so they often don't want to answer the question, "How long does my parent have?" By asking it the other way around, the question becomes easier to answer.

One way to ask what they mean when they say your parent needs a specific treatment is to ask, "Would this be Palliative care or Hospice care?"

Palliative Care is specialized medical care focused on providing relief from the symptoms and stress of the illness. The goal is to improve the quality of life for both the patient and those who care for the patient. Palliative care is based on the needs of the patient, not the likely course of the illness.

- Patients can continue to receive curative and therapeutic care such as chemotherapy, radiation, dialysis, and surgery while receiving palliative care.
- Palliative care is provided by a specially trained team of doctors, nurses, and other specialists who work together with a patient's other doctors.
- The palliative care team works together with the patient, their caregivers, and their family and inner circle. They communicate with all so that everyone is on the same page.
- Palliative care can be provided in any setting, such as hospitals, nursing homes, outpatient palliative care clinics, specialized clinics such as oncology, and at home.
- Palliative care services may include pain and symptom management.
- Care is coordinated with the current physicians and anyone else who is part of the healthcare team, and offers spiritual support and assistance with the development of the plan of care.
- Palliative care team members may also provide guidance with the completion of insurance forms and with making decisions about options regarding care and/or housing, and Advance Directives.

The cost of these services can be billed for the medical portion, such as nurses and physicians who support palliative care. Veterans may be eligible for palliative care through the Department of Veterans Affairs.

Be sure to check with your parent's doctor and healthcare plan to see what insurance will cover in your parent's particular situation.

Both palliative care and hospice care are focused on the needs of the patient and their quality of life, but hospice is specifically focused on the period closest to death.

Hospice Care focuses on quality of life when a cure is no longer possible, or the burdens of treatment outweigh the benefits. Hospice care is an interdisciplinary, team-oriented approach of expert medical care, pain management, and emotional and spiritual support expressly tailored to the patient's and family/inner circle's wishes and needs.

The goals of Hospice are:
- To keep the patient as pain-free as possible, with the loved ones nearby.
- Provide emotional support.
- Provide medications, medical supplies, and equipment.
- Coach caregivers on how to care for the patient.
- Deliver special services like speech and physical therapy when needed.
- Make short-term inpatient care available when pain or symptoms become too difficult to manage at home or when caregivers need respite time.
- Provides grief support, also known as bereavement support. Hospice is available if your aging parent's doctor thinks he/she has less than six months to live should their disease take its usual course.
- Talk with your parent's doctor if you think a hospice program might be helpful.

Most Hospice care patients are cared for in the place they call home, which is where most people would prefer to be. Although some hospice care is provided in hospitals, in-hospice facilities, or nursing homes.
- The day-to-day care of a person receiving hospice care in the home is provided by family, friends, or paid home health aides.

- The hospice team coaches caregivers on how to care for the patient and even provides respite care when caregivers need a break.
  - Respite care can be for as short as a few hours or for as long as several days.
  - Medicare covers up to five days of respite care at a time.

✍️ **Note: Patients will not receive curative treatment for their specific illness** but they will receive medications that enhance the quality of life, such as treatment for high blood pressure, anti-anxiety medications, and other medications to relieve any symptoms that they may have.

- Hospice care is available 'on call' seven days a week, 24 hours a day.
- Hospices are required to have nurses available to respond to a call for help. Some hospice programs have chaplains and social workers on call as well.
- It's important to know that hospice care in the home may require someone to be home with the patient 24 hours a day, seven days a week. If there is no one to do this, creative scheduling and good teamwork among friends, inner circle, and paid home health aides can overcome this problem.
- Members of the hospice staff will visit regularly to check on the patient, family, and caregivers. They will make sure that any symptoms are under control and give any needed care and services.

Respite Care - Medicare benefits pay for patient transport and up to five consecutive days of inpatient care at a Medicare-approved nursing facility or hospital.

- Respite care is available when a patient's medical condition warrants a short-term inpatient stay for pain or other symptoms that cannot be managed at home.
- For patients being cared for at home, some hospice services offer respite care to allow friends and family some time away from caregiving.

- Respite care can be given in up to 5-day periods, during which the patient is cared for either in the hospice facility or in beds that are set aside in nursing homes or hospitals.
- Families can plan a mini-vacation, go to special events, or simply get much-needed rest at home while having peace of mind.

When Death Occurs

When someone you love dies, the job of handling those personal and legal details may fall to you. It's a stressful task that can take a year or more to complete, all while you are grieving the loss.

You can't do it alone. Settling a deceased family member's affairs is not a one-person task. You'll need help from:

- Professionals like lawyers or CPAs, who can advise you on financial matters.
- A network of friends and relatives you can delegate tasks to or who you can lean on for emotional support.
- You may take the lead in planning the funeral and then hand off the financial details to the executor.
- To ensure everyone is aligned and coordinated during this challenging time, it can be helpful to have a checklist (*see below*) outlining all the tasks and considerations that need to be addressed. [4]

---

[4] https://www.aarp.org/home-family/friends-family/info-2020/when-loved-one-dies-checklist.html.

☑ Checklist: What to Do When Death Occurs

There are many things you will need to do immediately or in the next day or two.

- ☐ If your parent died at home, call the funeral home that you and your parent identified on page 183.
- ☐ If your parent died before you could choose a funeral home, either get a recommendation from a friend or locate one online. All funeral homes have 24-hour service, so do not hesitate to call immediately, even in the middle of the night.

Meet with the funeral director the next day to discuss the place, date, time, and type of service.

Provide the following items to the funeral director:

- ☐ Copy of birth certificate (*may not be required*). If you cannot locate a birth certificate, call the Bureau of Vital Statistics in the state in which your parent was born or call the County Recorder's Office if you know the county of their birth.
- ☐ Copy of Social Security card (*may not be required*).
- ☐ Burial insurance policy if one exists.
- ☐ Recent photo of deceased.
- ☐ Full set of clothing for the burial.
- ☐ Copy of deed to cemetery plot if one exists.
- ☐ Obituary information.
- ☐ Memorial information.
- ☐ Any papers necessary for an autopsy, if one is needed.
- ☐ Any papers necessary for cremation, if applicable.

✍ **Note:** *If the deceased's spouse is alive, they must sign the cremation papers. If there is not a living spouse, be sure to check if all adult children must sign the cremation agreement.*

- ☐ Request several official copies of the death certificate.

✍ **Note:** *Expect to pay $5 to $10 per copy.*

You will need official copies for:

1) All insurance policies
2) The attorney
3) The bank
4) The mortgage company, if applicable
5) The title company, if applicable

All other entities, like credit card companies, will accept copies.

Be sure to keep an official copy for yourself.

✍ **Note:** *It may take several weeks for official copies of the death certificate to arrive.*

- ☐ Locate the will.
- ☐ Notify your parent's attorney of death and request legal instructions.
- ☐ Locate documents of property and assets.
- ☐ Locate insurance companies.

✍ **Note:** *Notify insurance companies and request their requirements to receive benefits.*

- ☐ Notify close relatives and friends according to the list provided by your parent.

✍ **Note:** *If your parent corresponded with people outside of your personal acquaintance, you may want to write a short note and have it copied. You can then mail a personal notice. You could even suggest memorial donations to specific places if one wishes to donate.*

- ☐ Meet with a monument company, if applicable. Take page 185 with you.
- ☐ **LET OTHERS HELP YOU throughout this whole process!**

There are more things you will need to do, but you can do these in the weeks that follow:

- ☐ Keep a list of all flowers, gifts, and donations.
- ☐ Send thank-you notes and acknowledgments.
- ☐ Notify banks, credit unions, credit card companies, etc.
- ☐ If there is an estate, debts will need to be paid.
- ☐ Notify the Social Security office (1-800-772-1213).

✍ **Note:** *Return any Social Security checks that arrived after your parent's death. If the money is directly deposited, the bank will automatically return it when the government requests it.*

Questionnaire #25: Funeral Service Instructions

Use the following three questionnaires to determine what your parent's wishes are regarding his or her memorial service and burial.

Name of funeral home: _____

Phone: _____ Email: _____

Contact person: _____

Address: _____

Do you want cremation? ☐ Yes ☐ No

If yes, how do you want the remains handled?

- ☐ Burial Where _____
- ☐ Scattered Where _____
- ☐ Columbarium Where _____
- ☐ Other Where _____

If yes, do you want an open casket viewing before cremation?

- ☐ Yes ☐ No (*If yes, see instructions below*)

Do you want a funeral or memorial service? ☐ Yes ☐ No

If yes, where?

- ☐ Church ☐ Temple ☐ Synagogue
- ☐ Gravesite ☐ Funeral home ☐ Other

Name of your choice: _____

Location of your choice: _____

Name of person to officiate: _____

Phone: _____ Email: _____

Music selections: _____

_____

_____

_____

Bible verses, poems, spiritual readings, anecdotes: _____

_____

_____

_____

_____

Readers or speakers: _____

_____

_____

_____

_____

Do you want the casket open for viewing?   ☐ Yes   ☐ No

If yes, for whom? ☐ Family only   ☐ Everyone

Clothing choices: Jewelry choices:

_____   _____

_____   _____

Wedding rings: ☐ On   ☐ Off   Glasses: ☐ On   ☐ Off

Special instructions or wishes: _____

_____

Have you prepaid the funeral home? ☐ Yes   ☐ No
If no, what is the price beyond which your family should spend?

$_____

Questionnaire #26: Memorial Information

Name of cemetery: _____

Phone: _____ Email: _____

Address: _____

Do you already own a plot? ☐ Yes   ☐ No

Type of plot:

  ☐ Mausoleum   ☐ Ground Burial   ☐ Crypt   ☐ Urn/Niche

Location of deed to plot: _____

Do you want a headstone or other memorial marker? ☐ Yes   ☐ No

If yes, what would you like the marker to say?

_____

_____

_____

_____

Do you have any special instructions or thoughts about your memorial?

_____

_____

_____

_____

_____

Questionnaire #27: Obituary Information

Complete as many of these questions as your parent would like to have included in their obituary. Publishing an obituary is not required, but should be considered if your parent has many surviving friends.

Vital Statistics

Name: _____

Date of birth: _____ Place of birth: _____

Father's name: _____

Mother's name: _____ Maiden name: _____

Number of children: _____ Number of grandchildren: _____

Names of children:

_____ Where living _____

_____ Where living _____

_____ Where living _____

_____ Where living _____

Occupation (retired from)_____

Military Statistics

Branch of service: _____ Serial number: _____

Date entered service: _____ Place: _____

Date of separation from service: _____ Place: _____

Grade, rank, or rating: _____

Wars or conflicts served: _____

_____

Additional information: _____

_____

_____

Achievements or Accomplishments

Education: _____

Number of years: _____ Degrees: _____

Profession or vocation: _____

Civic or public offices held:

Office: _____ When: _____ Where: _____

Office: _____ When: _____ Where: _____

Other accomplishments you'd like noted: _____

_____

_____

_____

_____

_____

Notes: _____

_____

_____

Persons to Be Notified

Name: _____ Phone: _____

Address: _____

Relationship: _____

Name: _____ Phone: _____

Address: _____

Relationship: _____

Name: _____ Phone: _____

Address: _____

Relationship: _____

Name: _____ Phone: _____

Address: _____

Relationship: _____

Name: _____ Phone: _____

Address: _____

Relationship: _____

Name: _____ Phone: _____

Address: _____

Relationship: _____

Name: _____ Phone: _____

Address: _____

Relationship: _____

9

Protecting Your Aging Parent from Abusers, Predators and Opportunists

IN THIS CHAPTER:

- **Real Predator Story**
- **Elder Abuse**
- **Long-Term Effects of Elder Abuse**
- **Signs Your Parent Needs Help at Home**
- **Why Older Adults are Particularly Vulnerable**
- **Recognizing Different Types of Abuse**
- **Self-Neglect: What You Need to Know**
- **Signs and Symptoms of Self-Neglect**
- **Neglect: What You Need to Know**
- **Physical Abuse**
- **Emotional Abuse**
- **Financial Abuse and Exploitation**
- **Crimes of Opportunity**
- **Real Stories on Crimes of Opportunity**
- **Crimes of Predation**
- **Other Forms of Abuse**
- **What to do if You See Signs of Abuse**
- **How to Protect Your Elderly Parent from Abuse**
- **Resources**
- **Who are the Opportunists and Predators?**

Real Predator Story

Joyce is the daughter of Joe, an 88-year-old man who has been under the care of his wife, Joyce's 80-year-old stepmother, Marg for several years. It seemed as if Marg was rather closed off because she was not open and willing to discuss Joe's health and care needs with his family. Joyce contacted me to request an assessment and to provide Geriatric Care Management for Joe and Marg.

Joyce's main concerns were two-fold. She was contacted by her father's financial institution because he had requested all the money in his sole trust account be transferred to his wife's account. His wife had put Joe on the phone to make this request but it seemed suspicious since his wife had initially tried a couple of times to do this without his permission.

Also, Joe had been hospitalized with a significant brain injury due to a fall, but Marg did not notify Joyce. Joyce was unable to get any information regarding his care needs and medication. Marg told her she was not needed and would not allow Joyce access to any information from the hospital and his physicians.

Joyce contacted her attorney to discuss her concerns and her attorney recommended she call my company to get an assessment. Joyce called us and explained her concerns that her stepmother of nine years was trying to take money from Joe and seemed to be unclear about what his medical care needs were and was relying solely on her friend Betty to manage both their medical care and medication.

After our full neurocognitive assessment of Joe and Marg, and our interview with Betty, we discovered that Betty was helping Marg take money from Joe and was also stealing from Marg. Under Betty's care, both Marg and Joe were no longer following up on needed appointments with their physicians. Betty consistently failed to schedule Marg's diagnostic appointments. Betty also neglected to keep Joe's medical care current, allowing him to sleep 16-18 hours a day without being properly nourished or hydrated. In addition, Betty was giving both Joe and Marg the wrong medications. She was administering a blood thinner to both elderly adults which was dangerous, especially for Joe who had a brain injury and was not to have any blood thinners (Plavix).

Marg had been prescribed a blood thinner for 3 months, but during our assessment we discovered this order had been discontinued 6 months ago, and that Betty was still giving her this medication.

During this assessment process, we determined that Marg was a vulnerable adult who was relying on Betty to take care of her and her husband. Marg put Betty in charge of her Medical Power of Attorney and opened a Living Trust making Betty the Trustee and benefactor of her property and estate.

Marg was suffering from short-term memory loss and did not know or understand that she was being extorted by her "best friend" Betty.

We contacted Marg's family to request they work with an attorney to have the Medical Power of Attorney and a Durable Power of Attorney established so they could monitor their aunt's affairs.

We assisted both Marg's family and Joyce in replacing Betty with appropriate companions for this couple and stopped this abuse. This case was turned over to Marg's attorney who was able to assist Marg's family in recovering control and stabilizing the environment for Joe and Marg.

Joyce can now visit frequently and has been able to receive information on Joe's healthcare status.

Elder Abuse

"Elder abuse is a silent problem that robs seniors of their dignity, security and—in some cases—costs them their lives. Up to 5 million older Americans are abused every year, and the annual loss by victims of financial abuse is estimated to be at least $36.5 billion." [1]

Elder Abuse is a single or repeated act or lack of appropriate action.

(a) Occurs within any relationship in which there is an expectation of trust or dependence, and...

(b) Causes harm or distress to an older person

It is important to understand what Elder Abuse is because, at its core, elder abuse is "a violation of older adults' fundamental rights to be safe and free from violence and contradicts efforts toward improved well-being and quality of life in healthy aging". [2]

The National Institute on Aging (NIA) estimates that 1 in 10 elderly persons (those who are 60+) suffer from some type of abuse every year. Yet the signs of elder abuse often go unreported, and abusers go unpunished. These are sobering statistics that speak to the need to protect your aging parent from all forms of abuse. [3]

Abusers are both women and men. In almost 60% of elder abuse and neglect incidents, the perpetrator is a family member. Other perpetrators include staff at nursing homes and assisted living facilities, private duty caregivers, friends, guardians, and even professionals in the field of elder care like financial advisors.

Elder abuse includes physical abuse, emotional abuse, sexual abuse, financial exploitation, neglect, and abandonment. The websites below have information to help you understand in greater depth the problems of elder abuse and where to go for help:

---

[1] National Council on Aging, "Get the Facts on Elder Abuse," https://www.ncoa.org/article/get-the-facts-on-elder-abuse.

[2] Institute of Medicine and National Research Council, 2014, p. 1.

[3] https://www.nia.nih.gov/health/elder-abuse#effect.

- National Adult Protective Services Association - *napsa-now.org/aps-program-list/*
- National Long-Term Care Ombudsman Resource Center - *theconsumervoice.org/get_help*
- NCEA and United Nations resources

According to the National Institute on Aging, the most common warning signs of elder abuse are strange and sudden changes to an elderly loved one's mental, physical, or financial well-being.

Specific signs of elder abuse vary depending on what type of elder abuse is affecting the victim and can include:

- Injuries such as bruises, cuts, or broken bones
- Malnourishment or weight loss
- Poor hygiene
- Symptoms of anxiety, depression, or confusion
- Unexplained transactions or loss of money
- Withdrawal from family members or friends
- Financial irregularities: giving money to abusers, offering them gifts, or putting them in the will.

Elder abuse will not stop without intervention. Elder abuse is never acceptable and is considered a criminal act that needs to be reported to the authorities. Our responsibility is to help protect an elderly person who is being abused—please be sure you're stepping into this role of protector for your aging parent.

There are criminal penalties for the abusers. Most states have serious consequences for those who victimize older adults. Increasingly across the country, law enforcement personnel and prosecutors are receiving specialized training in identifying and addressing elder abuse, as well as utilizing criminal and civil legal mechanisms to hold these abusers accountable. Review state-specific elder justice laws on the Elder Abuse Guide for Law Enforcement (EAGLE) website. https://eagle.usc.edu/state-specific-laws

Long-Term Effects of Elder Abuse

Elder abuse can inflict serious harm on an individual's physical and mental health, destroy social and family relationships, cause devastating financial loss, and in some cases, contribute to premature death and more.

Any type of abuse can leave the victim feeling fearful and depressed. Additionally, they sometimes feel guilty, thinking the abuse is their fault. Adult Protective Service agencies can suggest counseling and support groups to help the abused person heal their emotional wounds.

STOP—TAKE ACTION:

STOP If an older adult is in immediate, life-threatening danger, call 9-1-1.

Anyone who suspects that an older adult is being mistreated should contact a local Adult Protective Services office, Long-Term Care Ombudsman, or thr police. *https://www.napsa-now.org/aps-program-list/*.

The National Council on Elder Abuse describes various scenarios and ways to get help, and more information is available from the Eldercare Locator online or by calling **1-800-677-1116**. *https://ncea.acl. gov/suspectabuse#gsc.tab=0*

Signs Your Parent Needs Help at Home

Aging is a process that does not occur suddenly. Small changes occur over time, and these changes can be subtle and difficult to notice immediately. To help you become more aware of any important signs that your parent needs help, use the following questionnaire.

These questions can help you recognize behaviors or circumstances that may indicate the potential presence of problems or concerning issues. The goal is to try to prevent a problem before it becomes a crisis.

Review and answer these questions to the best of your awareness:

- Do you find spoiled food that doesn't get thrown away in your parent's refrigerator?
- Is your parent eating a healthy diet?
- Are they losing weight?
- Is your parent's home dirty, with unwashed laundry and dishes piling up?
- Does their home have extreme clutter, stacks of unopened mail, or an overflowing mailbox (*late payment notices, bounced checks, and/or calls from bill collectors*)?
- Do your parents appear uncertain and confused when performing once-familiar tasks?
- Are they forgetting to take medications or taking more than the prescribed dosage?
- Do they have difficulty with walking, balance, and mobility, or trouble getting up from a seated position?
- Are you noticing a decline in grooming habits and personal care (*unpleasant body odor, strong smell of urine in the house, etc.*)?
- Do you see unexplained bruising?
- Do you notice your parent has changes in mood or extreme mood swings?
- Is your parent displaying a loss of interest in hobbies and activities?

Action:
- Identify any of the above situations.
- Be sure to follow-up on what is happening in your absence.
- Check that there are no behaviors or treatment by the caregivers, staff, or family caring for your parent that are causing stress, injury, or harm.
- Remember to Act if you are seeing any behaviors that are causing problems.

Why Older Adults are Particularly Vulnerable

There are many reasons why an elderly person can become a victim of abuse or exploitation. Victimization among older adults can occur if there is cognitive decline, an overly trusting nature, psychological vulnerability, social isolation, low inhibitions around risk-taking, and a lack of knowledge and information regarding fraud prevention.

Elderly people who are physically frail or have cognitive impairments are particularly vulnerable to becoming victims of abuse. Abusers typically target those who lack close family or friends nearby.

The most vulnerable adults for abuse and financial exploitation are those who depend on others for help with activities of everyday life such as bathing, dressing, taking medicine, meal preparation, shopping, and transportation to appointments.

Social isolation and/or loneliness also put these adults at a greater risk. We all need to connect or have contact with people. Being socially isolated can open the door to abuse by caregivers, scammers, and telemarketing fraud.

Unfortunately, older adults are disproportionately targeted by various kinds of fraud, which result in irreversible economic losses and great psychological distress.

Recognizing Different Types of Abuse

There are several different types of abuse, and it's important to recognize each of them so you can protect and help your parent. These include:

- Self-neglect
- Neglect
- Physical abuse
- Emotional abuse
- Financial abuse
- Sexual abuse
- Abandonment

- Healthcare fraud
- Crimes by opportunists
- Predators
- Scammers

Self-Neglect: What You Need to Know

The definition of self-neglect "is failure to provide for one's own essential needs" (*June 2020 -National Committee for the Prevention of Elder Abuse*).

- Self-neglect involves the elderly person who fails to meet their own essential physical, psychological, or social needs, which threatens their health, safety, and well-being. This includes failure to provide adequate food, clothing, shelter, and health care for one's own needs. (*National Committee for the Prevention of Elder Abuse*)
- The majority of self-neglecting older adults live alone, but self-neglect can occur when two or more people live in unsafe conditions and have unmet needs for basic care. As with other types of elder abuse, social isolation and lack of social support create risks for self-neglect.
- In older adults who become self-neglecting, hoarding behaviors are often associated with dementia or late-life depression.

What are the Signs and Symptoms of Self-Neglect?

Review this list and check any signs you are noticing or have been told by family or friends, during a recent visit.

- ☐ Your parent appears disheveled, in soiled and/or rumpled clothing.
- ☐ Your parent has a strong odor of feces or urine.
- ☐ Your parent's hair is matted or lice-infected.
- ☐ Your parent appears malnourished and/or dehydrated.
- ☐ Your parent is inappropriately attired for the climate.
- ☐ Your parent is living with serious untreated medical conditions and refusing treatment.

- ☐ Your parent's living environment is unsafe to exit or enter the residence due to hoarding/cluttering; pathways are not due to large amounts of clutter.
- ☐ Your parent is lacking fresh food, possessing only spoiled food, or not eating.

Report Safety Concerns and Self-Neglect if you are aware of any of the following signs:

- ☐ Inadequate heating, plumbing, or electrical service disconnected
- ☐ Animal feces in the home; infestation
- ☐ Residence is extremely dirty, filled with garbage, or very poorly maintained
- ☐ Not cashing monthly checks
- ☐ Needing medical care, but not seeking or refusing
- ☐ Refusing to allow visitors into the residence
- ☐ Giving away money inappropriately
- ☐ Dressing inappropriately for existing weather conditions

✍ **Note:**

Call Adult Protective Services or 9-1-1 if you observe the signs listed above but cannot convince your parent to get proper help.

Neglect: What You Need to Know

Another life-threatening abuse to an elderly person is neglect. The U.S. Justice Department notes that caregiver neglect is the most unreported type of abuse. Neglect occurs when there is no attempt to respond to the needs of the elderly person. These neglected needs may include physical, emotional, and social needs, or withholding food, medications, access to healthcare, a therapeutic device, or other physical assistance. Neglect exposes the older adult to the risk of physical, emotional, or mental harm.

What are the Signs and Symptoms of Neglect?

When visiting or interacting with your parent, review the checklist below. Do you have any concerns or see any signs that your elderly parent may not be receiving proper care?

- ☐ Is your parent getting adequate hydration daily? Is your parent suffering from dehydration? Adequate fluid is critical for health.
- ☐ Is your parent getting 2-3 meals per day? Or are you concerned your parent is not getting adequate nutrition? Failure to properly provide nutrition causes malnutrition.
- ☐ Are there signs of bed sores, fractures, contractures, over-medication, or poor personal hygiene?
- ☐ Are there any unattended or untreated health problems? Is your parent possibly suffering from a UTI (urinary tract infection)? It's very important to be sure your parent is not suffering from a UTI (urinary tract infection). If not sure, ask their physician to check.
- ☐ Are there hazardous or unsafe living conditions/arrangements (e.g., improper wiring, no heat, no running water, etc.)?
- ☐ Are there unsanitary and unclean living conditions (e.g., dirt, fleas, lice on person, bed bugs, soiled bedding, fecal/urine smell, inadequate clothing, etc.)?
- ☐ Does your parent report being mistreated, or are you discovering that they try to run away or leave where they're living every chance they get?
- ☐ Are your parent's finances being neglected?

Financial neglect occurs when an older adult's financial responsibilities such as paying rent or mortgage, medical expenses, or insurance, utility bills, or property taxes are ignored and the person's bills are not paid. Sometimes this neglect results in defaulting on the mortgage, losing insurance coverage, or creating a negative credit history.

✍ **Note:**

It is important to act immediately. Call Adult Protective Services or 9-1-1 if your parent is at risk of being neglected. Your parent's care needs must be met to avoid damage or harm to their well-being. There is no excuse for neglect - this is a criminal act!

Physical Abuse

What is physical abuse? If someone intentionally inflicts physical pain or injury on your aging parent this is physical abuse. This is a critical concern and must be stopped immediately as untreated bodily injury (wounds) can cause infections, delirium, and weakness leading to falls and/or eventual death.

What You Need to Know About Physical Abuse

It is very important to know how to recognize physical abuse and what to do about it. Your aging parent's health, well-being, and life depend on you acting if you suspect physical abuse.

Physical abuse can be any behavior that creates harm to your aging parent. Here are some examples:

- Hitting/slapping/choking
- Pushing/punching/kicking
- Burning, attempting to suffocate
- Intimidating, yelling, threats to hurt them
- Causing physical pain or injury in any way
- Restraining an older adult against their will (*such as locking them in a room or tying them to furniture*)

Signs and Symptoms of Physical Abuse

When visiting or interacting with your parent, do you see any of these signs or have any concerns that your parent may not be safe from harm?

☑ **Review the checklist below:** Place a check by any action you see that is/ has occurred:

- ☐ Bruises, black eyes, welts, marks, or any other physical signs of being subjected to punishment or being restrained.
- ☐ Bone fractures, broken bones, skull fractures.
- ☐ Open wounds, cuts, punctures, lacerations, and untreated injuries in various stages of healing.
- ☐ Sprains, dislocations, internal injuries/bleeding.
- ☐ Broken eyeglasses/frames or keeping assistive devices (cane, wheelchair, walker) away from your parent.
- ☐ Laboratory findings of medication overdose or underutilization of prescribed drugs.
- ☐ An elder's report of being hit, slapped, kicked, or mistreated.
- ☐ An elder's sudden change in behavior.
- ☐ Caregiver's refusal to allow visitors to see an elder person alone.

 STOP - TAKE ACTION!
    Remove your parent from harm immediately and report this abuse to Adult Protective Services and the police. If necessary, call 9-1-1.

Emotional Abuse

Often the elderly person who is being subjected to this type of abuse tends to be ashamed of what may be causing this action and blame themselves. This is very hurtful to the elderly person's sense of worth and dignity, and it can cause them to turn inward creating severe emotional problems such as depression, withdrawal, anxiety, and fear. This can—and often does—create the opportunity for neglect, physical abuse, and financial abuse.

What You Need to Know About Emotional Abuse

Emotional abuse is one of the harder abuses to detect, but it is very significant, especially if there are other types of abuse occurring concurrently. Emotional abuse is also called psychological abuse and examples are included in the following checklist.

Signs and Symptoms of Emotional Abuse

Is your aging parent experiencing any of the behaviors listed below? Review the checklist noting any action that you see, hear, or has been reported to you.

- ☐ Being subjected to verbal assaults, or yelling
- ☐ Being subjected to name-calling or cursing
- ☐ Yelling, threatening
- ☐ Being kept from seeing close friends and relatives
- ☐ Being subjected to threats of abuse, harassment, or intimidation
- ☐ Being subjected to shaming, demeaning words
- ☐ Being ignored repeatedly

Elderly adults who are suffering from emotional abuse often experience significantly higher levels of psychological distress than older individuals who have not experienced abuse.

STOP **STOP - TAKE ACTION!**

If you suspect your aging parent is being subjected to this type of abuse, stop it immediately. Report this to Adult Protective Services and remove the person who is abusing your parent from the home, or if your parent is in a facility, report this abuse to the person's supervisor with the request that he/she be removed from your parent's care immediately.

Financial Abuse and Exploitation

What is financial abuse? Elder financial abuse and exploitation is the illegal or improper use of an older adult's funds or property.

Financial abuse is becoming a widespread and hard-to-detect issue, with far-reaching and very real consequences. The FBI estimates that elderly Americans lose an estimated $3.5 billion to financial exploitation annually.

Financial abuse occurs whenever money or belongings are stolen from an older adult. This may include:

- Forging checks.
- Taking someone else's retirement or Social Security benefits.
- Using a person's credit cards and bank accounts without their permission.
- Changing names on a will, bank account, life insurance policy, or house/car title without permission.

Because there are so many ways financial information can be accessed and misused, financial abuse also extends past the theft of an older person's money or belongings and includes financial exploitation as well.

Financial Exploitation: What You Need to Know

The Federal Elder Justice Act, enacted in 2010, defines financial exploitation of the elderly as "the fraudulent or otherwise illegal, unauthorized, or improper act... that uses the resources of an elder person for monetary or personal benefit, profit, or gain, or that results in depriving an elder person the rightful access to, or use of, benefits, resources, belongings, or assets." *https://acl.gov/programs*

Signs and Symptoms of Financial Abuse/Exploitation

☑ Review and place a check next to any of these statements that are true.

- ☐ Your parent is taking a large amount of money out of the bank or other cash accounts.
- ☐ Your parent is making numerous withdrawals of smaller amounts.
- ☐ Your parent is writing a large check to someone you do not know.
- ☐ Your parent has changed power of attorney or beneficiaries on insurance or investment accounts.
- ☐ Your parent is bouncing checks or their bills are going unpaid.
- ☐ Your parent is making unusual or unnecessary purchases.
    - ☐ Your parent has agreed to make unnecessary home repairs.
    - ☐ Your parent is becoming **too close** to a person and is very influenced by their needs, opinions, or requests for financial security. This can be their companion, neighbor, salesman, or a clerk at a retail store, or grocery store, or bank.
    - ☐ Your parent's caregiver appears to be too interested in your parent's finances and is asking too many questions.
        1. If you have answered yes to any of these questions, you need to investigate your parent's finances with them.
        2. Within the elder law community, there is a great deal of concern about the burgeoning plague of elder financial abuse. According to a Consumer Financial Protection Bureau report, this problem is on the rise, costing seniors (*and their eventual heirs*) billions of dollars.

The Consumer Financial Protection Bureau broadly describes two different types of scenarios that are common within this arena.

Crimes of Opportunity

These instances of elder financial abuse are perpetrated by people who have access to the individual who is being victimized. This can be friends, neighbors, caregivers, acquaintances, and family members.

- Many seniors need are in need of assistance with their day-to-day needs, and caregivers are sometimes opportunists when it comes to taking advantage of their charges.
- This is a problem especially if the caregivers are independent contractors without oversight or supervision.

Real Stories on Crimes of Opportunity:

This is an example of opportunistic behavior without anyone monitoring how the aunt's care was being managed. The aunt was reluctant to challenge what these two women were doing for fear they would leave her.

I was contacted by Jessica who lived out of state and was concerned that her Aunt Lois had two caregivers that seemed to be spending her aunt's money on their own needs.

They would buy lunches for themselves and their guests when they took her aunt out for lunch six days a week. They were no longer making regular meals in the home for her. Her aunt would eat cereal, leftovers (if there were any, and frozen dinners. The weekly food bill was clearly more than what her aunt was eating, so these caregivers were also shopping for themselves using her aunt's cash or credit card.

✍ **Notes on the Real Stories on Crime of Opportunity:**

Jessica requested that her Geriatric Care Manager oversee her aunt's care and within one month the spending was reduced and her aunt's care was being better managed. Each caregiver was given a log with the instructions to write where they were taking the aunt and attach a receipt for any expenses. A menu was established which provided the list for grocery shopping. Meals were being prepared and served in her home.

The bank was notified not to give cash beyond the approved amount weekly, and to not issue any additional credit cards in her aunt's name. The Geriatric Care Manager reviewed monthly credit card statements and bank statements to ensure that no unnecessary spending was occurring.

It turns out this was just the tip of the iceberg. In addition to being financially abused by these two caregivers, her financial advisor was also taking advantage of the aunt's lack of oversight of her finances.

Crimes of Predation

There are identity thieves, con men, and scam artists out there always looking for an easy mark. It is not uncommon for these criminal types to target the elderly under the assumption that they are particularly vulnerable.

Unfortunately, some professionals who the elderly trust can also exploit their relationship and take advantage of their vulnerable clients. Undue influence is the underlying problem.

✍ **Note:**

To avoid opportunists taking advantage of vulnerable adults, it is best to have someone monitor or supervise the caregivers and trusted professionals in their lives.

> ✍ **Note:**
>
> If you have concerns or questions about the appropriateness of your elder parent's Financial Advisor, always get a second opinion before allowing any financial decision to be made. But if you were unaware until after the decisions were made, contact FINRA if you believe your parent's account may have been mishandled by the broker.
>
> **Call 844-57-HELPS (844-574-3577) FINRA**
>
> (*The Financial Industry Regulatory Authority*)

Websites you can look up for more information:

1) **FINRA** recommends that your parent add a trusted contact person to a brokerage account to prevent financial exploitation, and to ask the broker right away about any unclear transactions. If their response is inadequate or suspicious, contact the brokerage firm's manager or compliance department, and keep files of the communications.

2) Brokerage firms are now permitted to place a temporary hold on a securities transaction when exploitation is suspected. If the brokerage does not resolve the situation, you can send the complaint to FINRA for investigation and/or referral.

FINRA

1735 K Street, NW

Washington, DC 20006

301-590-6500

https://www.finra.org/investors/need-help/file-a-complaint

3) **Administration for Community Living (ACL) Protecting Rights and Preventing Abuse**

4) ACL develops programs for abuse prevention, helping people in abusive situations, and supporting people who have experienced abuse to help them recover. *https://acl.gov/*

5) **CFPB Office of Financial Protection for Older Americans**
   The Consumer Financial Protection Bureau (CFPB) is a government agency that makes sure banks, lenders, and other financial companies treat seniors fairly.
   https://www.consumerfinance.gov/consumer-tools/educator-tools/resources-for-older-adults/

6) **Department of Justice's Elder Justice Initiative**
   The Elder Justice Initiative supports the Department's enforcement efforts to combat elder abuse, neglect and financial fraud and scams that target seniors. *https://www.justice.gov/elderjustice*

7) **Federal Trade Commission Scam Alerts**
   The FTC protects consumers by stopping unfair, deceptive or fraudulent practices by investigating and filing lawsuits.
   https://consumer.ftc.gov/features/scam-alerts

 Note:

More detailed information about how opportunists, scammers, and predators operate, and what to do about it, is available at the end of this chapter.

Other Forms of Abuse

In addition to physical, emotional, and financial abuse and neglect, other forms of abuse include:

Abandonment

This form of abuse occurs when a caregiver leaves an older adult who needs help alone without planning for their care. It is a failure to provide any care or services to meet the elderly person's medical, health, daily living, or safety needs.

There is no oversight from a concerned or responsible person to assure that the elderly person is safe, their needs are met, or even that there is adequate housing.

Sexual Abuse

This involves a caregiver forcing an older adult to watch or be part of sexual acts. Sexual abuse includes touching, fondling, intercourse, or any other sexual activity with an older adult who is unable to understand, is unwilling to consent, or is threatened or physically forced.

Healthcare Fraud

Healthcare fraud can be committed by doctors, hospital staff, or other health care workers. It includes overcharging, billing for services not received, or billing for services multiple times. The family of the older adult and caregivers should keep an eye out for this type of fraud.

Websites for more information on types of abuse:

- https://ncea.acl.gov/home#gsc.tab=0
- https://www.nia.nih.gov/health/elder-abuse
- https://www.ncoa.org/article/get-the-facts-on-elder-abuse

What to do if You See Signs of Abuse

Any type of mistreatment can leave the abused person feeling fearful and depressed. Sometimes the victim thinks the abuse is his or her fault, and many older adults are afraid that if they make a report, it will get back to the abuser and make the situation worse. Elder abuse can lead to early death, harm to physical and psychological health, destruction of social and family ties, devastating financial loss, and more, so you must step in if you see any signs of abuse.

 Note:

If you think someone you know is being abused physically, emotionally, financially, sexually, or neglected, be sure to explore what might be happening with to them.

- Talk with him or her when the two of you are alone. You could say you think something is wrong and you're worried.
- Offer to take him or her to get help—for instance, to a local Adult Protective Services agency, their physician, or their clergy—to talk about what is happening.
- Most states require that social workers, nurses, doctors, and lawyers report elder mistreatment.
- Family and friends can also report it. Do not wait. Help is available.
- You do not need to prove that abuse is occurring. That will be the responsibility of the professional who is investigating.

If you think someone is in imminent danger, call 9-1-1 or go to your local police to get help right away.

How to Protect Your Elderly Parent from Abuse?

These are strategies to keep your elderly parent from falling prey to scammers, predators, and opportunists:

1) Stay informed about current scams and discuss these with your elderly parent. You can get up-to-date information by checking with the following organizations:
   https://consumer.ftc.gov/features/scam-alerts
   - Federal Trade Commission – for information on Covid contact tracing scams *https://www.ftc.gov/coronavirus*
   - Federal Communications Commission – for information on Covid-related consumer scams *https://www.fcc.gov/covid-scams*
   - Fraud.org – for general helpful information about fraud, and to report a complaint *http://www.fraud.org/*

2) It's also important to keep in close contact with your elderly parents to prevent them from feeling lonely. Visit regularly, if possible, and stay connected over the telephone or video chats when visiting in person is not possible.

3) Remind your parent not to respond to messages or calls from unfamiliar senders/callers.

4) Remind your parent that they should discuss making any online purchases related to computer viruses or sharing financial information with someone they know and trust.

5) Remind your parent to be aware of and cautious of clicking on any links in texts or emails that appear to be questionable.
   - Online fraud is increasing across all age groups, so it's important to pay attention to any potential schemes they may have fallen prey to.
   - Notice if they're excited to share a service they were alerted to—be sure to get details and the contacts.

6) If your elderly parent is online, share with them how it is risky to create connections through social media and online with people they do not have relationships with offline.
   - Remind them that it is quite common for schemers to create fake profiles and pretend to be another person or act on behalf of a well-known, trustworthy company.

IMPORTANT!

If your parent becomes the victim of fraud, be supportive.

- Do not victimize them again by making them feel foolish and ashamed.
- Do not blame them.
- Being reassuring and sensitive will help your parent feel more comfortable reporting the situation to authorities.

Family and caregivers of the elderly need to be aware of predators looking to take advantage of the vulnerable older population. Several scams related to Covid-19 directed at the senior age group have surfaced. Being frightened by the pandemic and feeling lonely from social distancing can make your parent a prime target and susceptible to fraud.

Resources

For more information about elder abuse and where to get help connect with these organizations:

Eldercare Locator
800-677-1116 (toll-free)
eldercarelocator@n4a.org
https://eldercare.acl.gov

Consumer Financial Protection Bureau
Office for Older Americans
855-411-2372 (toll-free)
olderamericans@cfpb.gov
www.consumerfinance.gov/practitioner-resources/resources-for-older-adults

National Adult Protective Services Association
202-370-6292
https://www.napsa-now.org/aps-program-list/

National Center on Elder Abuse
855-500-3537 (toll-free)
ncea-info@aoa.hhs.gov
https://ncea.acl.gov/

National Elder Fraud Hotline
833-FRAUD-11 for 833-372-8311
https://stopelderfraud.ovc.ojp.gov

U.S. Department of Justice

202-514-2000 • 800-877-8339 (TTY/toll-free)

elder.justice@usdoj.gov

https://www.justice.gov/elderjustice/find-support-elder-abuse

Online Financial Loss quiz: *www.justice.gov/elderjustice/roadmap*

Who are the Opportunists and Predators that Prey on the Elderly?

Financial abuse is a problem on the rise, costing seniors (*and their eventual heirs*) billions of dollars, and there are many reasons for this:

- Older adults are often isolated and lonely; they may be a widow or widower, and they may have fewer friends.
- They know their children may be trying to help, but these children are often busy with their own daily affairs. (*They are often in the sandwich generation—with both elderly parents and children to look after.*)
- The elderly adult's physical and cognitive functions are generally not as good as when they were younger. As a result, elderly adults are often more vulnerable and may need to rely on others to meet their needs.

All of this creates a perfect victim for opportunists and predators to take advantage of the elderly person.

Within the elder law community, there is a great deal of concern about the apparently burgeoning plague of elder financial abuse.

 Be on the Lookout for Predators!

The Consumer Financial Protection Bureau provides the four typical steps used by professional predators to target seniors. This is how they set up elderly adults:

Step 1: They acquire an audience by appealing to a senior's desire to save money

Professional financial predators must first get a captive audience of willing seniors together.

- Watch out for the "Free Lunch" or "Free Seminar" that promises free and important information on "Living Trusts," "Reverse Mortgages," or "Financial/Money-Saving Opportunities."

Not all these opportunities are the prelude to abuse, but it is important that your vulnerable parent not go to these alone.

- You need to caution your elderly parent not to sign anything until their attorney, financial advisor, or you review it.

Step 2: They find out what the senior owns

The financial predator finds out what the senior owns in terms of property, savings, annuities, and equity in their home and other assets.

- This is accomplished by handing out questionnaires at the "Free Lunch" or "Free Seminar" that will be used to determine which attendees will later be targeted for financial exploitation at a sales presentation.

Step 3: They incite fear, causing a senior to want to move their assets

The financial predator creates a need for the senior to move their assets or buy an expensive insurance product—like an annuity that pays the predator a huge commission.

- This is usually accomplished by creating fear and insecurity about one's life savings.

- The scammer will tell your parents or elderly relative he will "protect your estate" and "secure it for your children."
- Your parent might be told that "you will go into a nursing home and outlive your money" or that they need to "avoid probate" or "qualify for Medi-Aid" or a host of other doom-and-gloom scenarios to create enough fear and concern to induce your parent to comply with the predator's wishes.

Step 4: They encourage the liquidation of assets, and move them to commission-based products

In the final step, the financial predator closes the deal by having your parent move his or her money somewhere where the predator earns a commission.

- Watch out for IRA rollovers, direct cash purchases, reverse mortgages, consulting fees for assistance to qualify for a government product, or the purchase of an expensive annuity.
- All of these transactions can be used for an inappropriate or unsuitable purpose.

 Note:
Many senior citizens can begin to lose sound decision-making capabilities as they reach an advanced age.

Here are a few steps you can take to protect your elderly parent from abuse:

- Professional guidance is the key if you want to steer clear of elder financial abuse and other abuses that can involve vulnerable senior citizens.
- It is important to discuss the legal aspects of protecting your elderly parents with an experienced professional by arranging a consultation with a licensed elder law attorney.
  - They can assist you and your parent with planning for the future.
  - Incapacity planning is an important part of any comprehensive plan. An elder law attorney can help you set up advance directives, trusts, a will, and special trusts, if needed.

10

Caregiver Care: Taking Care of You

IN THIS CHAPTER:

- **Real Story About a Caregiver in Distress**
- **Ten Signs of Caregiver Stress**
- **Checklist: Symptoms of Stress**
- **Checklist: Demands on Your Time and Energy**
- **Managing Stress**
- **Getting Help**
- **Dealing with Feelings**
- **Ways to Reduce the Effect of Stress**
- **Activities for the Soul: Enhancing Spirituality**

Real Story About a Caregiver in Distress

One of my clients was watching over her father who was absolutely resistant to anyone providing his care. He would not let her hire anybody to help with the caregiving tasks, and just barely tolerated us. But he knew that his daughter needed us whenever he had to go to a doctor and set up medicines.

Our client was trying to take care of her father, but clearly, she was showing extreme signs of fatigue because she was just a shadow of herself. There was clearly something wrong. We strongly encouraged her to let us put in a temporary caregiver and recommended she go to her physician ASAP. She was put in the hospital to get a workup and it turned out she had Lupus, which had been exacerbated because of the level of care she was having to provide to her father. She was so distressed. The doctor gave her a treatment plan.

With her permission, we called her family and said, "Your father needs to be placed, or somebody has to come and provide the care because it's literally making your sister very ill. Even if you can't physically be here, you can all share in providing some of the costs to get help for your parent and her.

Sometimes caregivers may have a strong underlying need to feel needed or loved, or they may view caregiving as an opportunity to express appreciation towards their parent. But it is important not to take things too far, to the point where your own well-being is compromised.

Many people caring for an aging parent do so out of a place of compassion. The desire to do the right thing is understandable. However, if you're neglecting your health and personal life, and there's an overall lack of balance, that's a clear warning sign that needs to be addressed. It's crucial to make sure you're also taking care of yourself amidst the caregiving responsibilities.

It is a very difficult time for you when your parent begins to need help. You're getting actively engaged in a new and different path with your parent. It's time to pull together the information you need, but you can't do this alone.

Take note of the entirety of the situation with the assessments provided in this book and then bring in professionals and others that can help you put together a plan of care. You need a plan for your parent. Then you need a plan for your future care, using the tools in this book.

This chapter is dedicated to you, the caregiver.

It provides information and support for taking care of yourself and getting the help you need while you are a caregiver of your elderly parent or family member.

Caregiving is not a role to be taken lightly. It can be incredibly demanding, as it requires hard work and a significant amount of energy. In the process, you may find yourself stretched too thin, struggling to juggle the responsibilities of your job, other family members, friends, social obligations, and even making time for your self-care. The demands of caregiving can easily consume you if you don't proactively maintain a healthy balance.

Some of you will experience the sad realization that Mom or Dad (or even your spouse) is no longer the same person you knew when they were younger. The emotional trauma of watching your aging relative decline can create your own need for compassionate understanding. This is a great loss of a very special relationship, one that holds a variety of meanings, experiences, and emotions.

Trying to provide care while grieving this loss is a very complicated task, one fraught with love, anger, frustration, sadness, and guilt. These feelings are normal and only human. It is important to recognize your feelings, and not try to suppress them.

You may be inclined to focus on the needs and the feelings of your aging parent, unfortunately at the expense of your feelings. This is a natural reaction, especially if you see someone you love suffering. Most people want to do whatever they can to make it better for them, and the result is often suppressing your feelings and emotions so you can do what is needed and offer the best care you can.

Please take time to review this section anytime you feel the need to take a break. Now is the time to think about what you need and want. This chapter is written for all of you-there are no two situations or caregiving relationships that are the same. The suggestions presented here are general in nature-use them to fit your circumstances. Adapt them, expand them, or pass over the ones that aren't relevant.

Do What is Right for You

Remember, it is important to acknowledge your feelings. All your feelings are valid, there is no right or wrong. You are human, and you have the right to fully feel whatever it is you are experiencing. It's also important to know that help is available! Here is a list of resources you may want to consult:

- The Alzheimer's Association (www.alz.org) can help you learn more about Alzheimer's disease and other dementias and find local support services. Their 24/7 helpline can be reached at 800-272-3900.
- The Michael J. Fox Foundation for Parkinson's Research (*www.michaeljfox.org*) offers information for people living with Parkinson's disease and research updates. They can be reached at 800-708-7644.
- The Parkinson's Foundation (*www.parkinson.org*) is a nonprofit organization providing information and resources for diagnosed individuals, families, and health professionals. Reach the Parkinson's Foundation at 800-473-4636 or helpline@parkinson.org.
- The National Institute on Aging's Age-Related Dementias Education and Referral (ADEAR) Center offers information and free print publications about Alzheimer's and related dementias for families, caregivers, and health professionals. ADEAR Center staff answer telephone, email, and written requests and make referrals to local and national resources. Find them at 800-438-4380, adear@nia.nih.gov, or *www.nia.nih.gov/alzheimers*.
- Explore the Alzheimers.gov portal for information and resources on Alzheimer's and related dementias from across the federal government.
- Lewy Body Dementia Association: 404-935-6444, 800-539-9767 (toll-free LBD Caregiver Link), *www.lbda.org*.

- Lewy Body Dementia Resource Center: 833-LBDLINE, *lewybodyresourcecenter.org*
- Mayo Clinic: *www.mayoclinic.org/patient-care-and-health-information*
- MedlinePlus National Library of Medicine: *www.medlineplus.gov*
- The National Institute of Mental Health Information Resource Center Phone: 866-615-6464 or live chat online: Talk to a representative by email: nimhinfo@nih.gov or by mail: National Institute of Mental Health: Office of Science Policy, Planning, and Communications 6001 Executive Boulevard, Room 6200, MSC 9663 Bethesda, MD 20892-9663.

An overload can create stress that can ultimately can make you sick and unable to care for yourself, let alone your parent.

However, when immersed in the daily business of providing care you often ignore your own symptoms. An overload of stress is harmful to the body, psyche, and soul.

Some of the activities on the following list will be meaningful and helpful to you. Some you may be able to find time to do by yourself, and some you may benefit from doing with your aging parent.

This is best illustrated by a short allegory:

Once upon a time, there were two frogs. The first frog was dropped into a pot of hot water. The frog felt the intense heat and immediately jumped out, saving his life.

The second frog was dropped into a pot of cool water that was placed on a burner set on low heat. Slowly (one or two degrees at a time) the temperature increased, but never so much that the frog was uncomfortable. He got used to the increase in temperature and therefore remained in the pot. The frog stayed in the pot until the temperature was hot enough to boil him.

What is the message of this story? It is often the gradual, hardly perceptible stressors in our lives, lifestyle, and character that can create problems for us!

Classic physical symptoms are headaches, gastrointestinal problems, sleep disturbances, and back or shoulder tension. Isolation from friends, guilt, depression, and family conflict can creep in and cause emotional exhaustion. Given the burdens of decision-making, increased responsibilities, and the disruption of one's own life, it is hardly a wonder that caregivers often feel stressed.

The information in this chapter is provided to help you recognize and relieve the signs and symptoms of stress. To ignore them would be detrimental to both you and your aging relative. Taking positive steps to manage stress can help protect you from becoming exhausted and burned out. You can do so by looking at the following topics in this chapter.

- Ten Signs of Caregiver Stress
- Checklist: Symptoms of Stress
- Checklist: Demands on Your Time and Energy
- Managing Stress: What You Need to Know
- Getting Help
- Ways to Reduce the Effects of Stress
  - Relaxation Technique: How to Elicit the Relaxation Response
  - Relaxation Technique: The Relaxation Response During Exercise
  - Relaxation Technique: A Breathing Exercise
  - Relaxation Technique: Progressive Muscle Relaxation

Ten Signs of Caregiver Stress

Excessive much stress can be damaging to both you and the person you are caring for. The following stress indicators can lead to more serious health problems. If you experience any of them frequently or simultaneously, pay attention. Learn to recognize signs of stress in yourself, since taking care of yourself is the most important aspect of being an effective caregiver.

1) Denial about the illness and its effect on the person who has been diagnosed.
   I know my mom is going to get better.
2) Anger at the loss of your parent's ability to function and the demands on you.
   If he asks me that question one more time, I will scream.
3) Social Withdrawal from friends and activities that once brought pleasure.
   I don't care about getting together with the neighbors anymore.
4) Anxiety about facing another day and what the future holds.
   What happens when he needs more care than I can provide?
5) Depression causing a break in your spirit and affecting your ability to cope.
   I don't care anymore.
6) Exhaustion making it nearly impossible to complete necessary tasks.
   I'm too tired for this.
7) Sleeplessness caused by a never-ending list of concerns.
   What if she wanders out of the house and hurts herself?
8) Irritability that leads to moodiness and triggers negative responses and reactions.
   Leave me alone!
9) Lack of concentration making it difficult to perform familiar tasks.
   I was so busy I forgot we had an appointment.
10) Health problems taking their toll, both mentally and physically.
   I can't remember feeling good.

☑ Checklist: Symptoms of Stress

Stress takes its toll on us in many ways. Any one of the symptoms in any of the categories below can indicate that you are suffering from stress.

Check any of the symptoms you have experienced recently:

Physical	Emotional
☐ Headaches	☐ Anxiety
☐ Teeth grinding	☐ Frustration
☐ Fatigue	☐ Nervousness
☐ Insomnia	☐ Depression
☐ Backaches	☐ Worrying
☐ Stomach Problems	☐ Tension
☐ Colds	☐ Mood Swings
☐ Neck Aches	☐ Easily Discouraged
☐ Shoulder Pains	☐ Crying Spells
☐ Increased Use of Drugs	☐ Irritability
Mental	**Social**
☐ Forgetfulness	☐ Isolation
☐ Poor Concentration	☐ Loneliness
☐ Low Productivity	☐ Lashing Out
☐ Negative Attitude	☐ Clamming Up
☐ Confusion	☐ Lower Sex Drive
☐ No New Ideas	☐ Nagging
☐ Lethargy	☐ Less Contact with Friends
☐ Boredom	

Action:

How is your stress revealing itself? Make a list of the symptoms you are experiencing now.

_____

_____

_____

☑ Checklist: Demands on Your Time and Energy

You have many demands on you, your time, and your energy, especially if you are a caregiver, spouse, parent, child, and employee/employer. This checklist will help you identify who and what places demand your time and energy.

Make blank copies for completion by any person who is involved or willing to be involved in the care of your aging parent. Once completed this list becomes an excellent tool to help identify the time each person has to give to caring for your aging parent.

Check any item that applies to your current situation:

- ☐ Married
- ☐ Single
- ☐ Children under the age of 18
- ☐ Adult children living at home
- ☐ Adult children out of the home
- ☐ Grandchildren
    - ☐ Living in your home
    - ☐ Living out of your home
- ☐ Aging parents or in-laws
    - ☐ Living in your house
    - ☐ Living in your community, but not your home
    - ☐ Living in your state
    - ☐ Living out of state
- ☐ Career or job
- ☐ Attending school
- ☐ Homemaker/housekeeper
- ☐ Gardener/groundskeeper
- ☐ Relatives who expect regular letters, emails, phone calls
- ☐ Social life with friends
- ☐ Church or synagogue responsibilities
- ☐ Clubs or organizations

- ☐ Officer or special duties
- ☐ Other _____
- ☐ Other _____
- ☐ Other _____

 Note:

This list of people and activities represents who you are and what is important to you. Look closely at what you have checked. How do you spend your time? What is important to you? If you feel your energy and time are too stretched, you may need to do a time study to reallocate how you choose to spend your time.

Managing Stress: What You Need to Know

This section is designed to help you relieve and manage the stress of caregiving. The focus is on how to survive stress.

We are forever changing and forever being recreated. What a wonderful, empowering thought! Through our attitudes, beliefs, behaviors, and lifestyle choices we define who we are and what we will become.

Being a healthy caregiver is possible if you choose to take care of yourself as well as you take care of your family, friends, and employer/employees. How you feel and the choices you make each day are connected.

Here is a scale of how you feel. Mark how you feel on a typical day:

I am as healthy as I can be.	Life is wonderful.	I feel great.	I feel good.	I don't feel so good.	I feel terrible.	I've never felt so bad.	I doubt if I will make it through the day.	I feel pain, needless suffering, devastated.

Take Action:
- Now look at the scale again.
- Circle how you would like to feel on a typical day.

How can you move to where you want to be stress-wise?
List some ideas or choices you need to make to create a better typical day.

_____

_____

_____

Your daily choices make up your lifestyle. Your day-in and day-out choices determine how you feel and how stressed you are. Making any changes can affect your stress level.

What is important for you to recognize as a caregiver is what behaviors and choices are impacting your lifestyle now and need to be controlled or changed for you to remain whole, happy, and less stressed.

Getting Help

One way to relieve stress is to ensure that you have help with providing care for your aging parent. Identifying the resources and people who can help you is a critical part of relieving stress and maintaining a balanced lifestyle.

The people you looked to for information during the assessment process may also be the people who will lend help and support in caregiving. Generally, it will be your family that will form the nucleus of support and help.

When it is time to initiate actual caregiving, call a family meeting. If possible, involve everyone in the family, even those who may not be as invested as you are in developing a care plan. Sometimes it is best to have the session led by a social worker or geriatric care manager, especially if history shows conflict among some family members.

Have each family member complete the "Checklist: Demands on your Time". It will help all of you look at each person's commitments and see what takes his or her energy, interest, and time. Not everyone will be on equal footing. Remember, some people are good at paperwork, some are good communicators, some may be better at researching online, some may be better able to contribute financially, and some may be just good at encouraging. There will be a role for everyone. Be sensitive and realistic, but help each one find a role in the care process.

Once you have involved the whole family, remember to look to external (outside the family) support you identified in the assessment phase. Some people may be available for part-time help, socialization, or moral support. Always accept any help that is offered. Sharing responsibility and accepting help is a part of taking good care of you, the primary caregiver, as well as your aging parent.

Dealing with Feelings

Usually, the aging parent will rely primarily on one adult child, who becomes the primary caregiver. If you are in the role of primary caregiver, it is important to consider the feelings of the other adult children and family of the aging parent. Remember the family and siblings may view this shift in your relationship with the aging parent as threatening or hurtful, or have feelings of being excluded (even if they could not realistically be the primary caregiver).

Remember that each family member has a relationship with your aging parent that is unique and special. Each has feelings about the past that may sometimes be warm and positive, and sometimes be painful and negative. Generally, these feelings don't surface until the adult child becomes the direct caregiver or determines they are not able or willing to become the direct care giver. Frequently the intensity of these feelings surprises the adult child and they don't know how to deal with them. Family members can help each other cope with these feelings, if they agree to discuss these feelings openly and honestly without blame, accusations, or guilt. We can't always help how we feel, but we can choose how we react to how we feel.

As the primary caregiver, it's important to have open conversations with all your siblings and other family members. Discuss how they feel about the situation and get their input on what they believe the aging parent's needs are. This will allow each person to feel involved and help to decrease any negative reactions or feelings.

Of course, all relevant family members should be included in the process of decision-making whenever realistic and possible. However, it should be understood and agreed upon that the final decision rests with the primary caregiver. It is too easy to recommend solutions if you are not the one who must carry them out, so be mindful and considerate of the family member who will implement the caregiving tasks. All is not as simple and easy to resolve as it seems from afar.

Ways to Reduce the Effect of Stress

Caregiving, whether direct or indirect, can be a major source of stress in someone's life. The following are some suggestions to help you manage stress as you try to balance your time and energy between your various responsibilities.

1) Eat at least one balanced meal a day.
2) Get seven to eight hours of sleep (*or whatever number of hours you require*) at least four nights a week.
3) Have a network of friends and acquaintances you can talk to.
4) Have at least one friend or relative you can confide in about personal matters.
5) Take care of your own health.
6) Limit or eliminate smoking, alcoholic beverages, and caffeine-rich drinks.
7) Exercise daily.
8) Talk openly about your feelings when you are angry or hurt.
9) Attend a social gathering or activity that you enjoy at least once a week.
10) Organize your time - make lists you can use to check off tasks you have accomplished.

11) Find some quiet time for yourself each day.

12) Give and receive affection regularly.

13) Laugh and find humor in daily events and tasks.

 Note:

There are a variety of techniques to manage stress. Most stress reduction techniques are designed to promote one thing — relaxation. The following pages present some of the various methods that we have seen work. What is most important is that you choose a technique and practice it. Measure your success not by how well you perform the technique, but rather by how it makes you feel.

Relaxation Technique: How to Elicit the Relaxation Response

Here is some general advice on the regular practice of the relaxation response:

Try to find 10 to 20 minutes in your daily routine; before breakfast is a good time. Arrange your life so you won't have any distractions. Put your phone on Do Not Disturb and ask someone else to watch the kids (if you have any) or your aging parent. Track the time by glancing periodically at a clock or watch (but don't set the alarm). Commit yourself to a specific length of practice and try to stick to it.

There are several approaches to eliciting the relaxation response. Here is one standard set of instructions used in the Mind/Body Medical Institute:

Step 1.

Pick a focus word or short phrase that's firmly rooted in your belief system. For example, a Christian person could use a prayer, such as the opening words of Psalm 23, "The Lord is my shepherd." Other words could be Peace, Love, One, Joy, Shalom.

Step 2.

Sit quietly in a comfortable position.

Step 3.

Close your eyes.

Step 4.

Relax your muscles.

Step 5.

Breathe slowly and naturally, repeating your focus word or phrase silently as you exhale.

Step 6.

Throughout the process, assume a passive attitude. Don't worry about how well you're doing. When other thoughts come into your mind, simply say to yourself, "Oh well," and gently return to the repetition.

Step 7.

Continue for the number of minutes you allotted. You may open your eyes to check the time, but remember, do not use an alarm. When you finish, sit quietly for a minute or two, at first with your eyes closed and later with your eyes open. Do not stand until a minute or two has passed. Practice this technique once or twice a day.

Relaxation Technique: The Relaxation Response During Exercise

This relaxation response can be elicited during walking or jogging by following these steps:

1. Get into sufficiently good condition so that you can jog or walk without getting excessively out of breath.

2. Do your usual warm-up exercises before you walk or jog.

3. As you exercise, keep your eyes fully open, but attend to your breathing. After you fall into a regular pattern of breaths, focus on its in-and-out rhythm. As you breathe in, say to yourself, "In." When you exhale, say to yourself, "Out." In effect, the words "in" and "out" become your mental device or focus words, in the same way that you use your personal focus words or phrases with other relaxation response methods. If this in/out rhythm is uncomfortable for you (you might feel that your breathing is too fast or too slow),

focus on something else. For example, you can become aware of your feet hitting the ground, silently repeating "one, two, one, two," or "left, right, left, right." There is, of course, nothing wrong with focusing on a faith-oriented word or phrase during exercise. In fact, it could make your exercise more satisfying.

4. Remember to maintain a passive attitude. Simply disregard disruptive thoughts. When they occur, think to yourself, "Oh, well," and return to your repetitive focus word or phrase.

5. After you complete your exercise, return to your normal after-exercise routine.

Relaxation Technique: A Breathing Exercise

The best way to breathe is diaphragmatically.

1. For at least five minutes, focus on your breath without trying to manipulate it in any way.

2. Then, with your mouth closed, inhale quietly through your nose to a silent count of four.

3. Hold your breath for four seconds.

4. Finally, exhale audibly through your mouth for four seconds.

5. Work to make your breathing deeper, slower, quieter, and more regular. Your belly should expand like a balloon as you inhale. As you exhale, allow your diaphragm to deflate, then your rib cage, then your chest.

6. Repeat the entire exercise four times, twice daily.

Relaxation Technique: Progressive Muscle Relaxation

In progressive muscle relaxation, you progress through your body, tensing and then relaxing each major muscle group. You can begin either from your toes up to your head or vice versa. This technique helps you experience the difference in feeling when your muscles are tensed and relaxed.

This technique is best done lying on your back on a firm but soft surface, such as a thick carpet or workout mat. (A bed is too soft-you are likely to glide off to sleep.) It can also be done in any large chair that supports your head and neck.

To begin: Lie on your back with your arms along your sides. Loosen any uncomfortably tight clothing. It is best to take off your shoes. Have someone read you these instructions or make a tape for yourself.

Read the instructions out loud at a slow but not monotonous pace. The general idea is to tense up each area of your body, and then consciously relax it, starting at the top of your head or with your toes.

1) Start by tensing as many muscle groups you can throughout your body. Tighten your feet and legs, your arms and hands, clench your jaw, and contract your stomach. Hold the tension while you sense the feeling of strain and tightness. Now release this tension and notice the difference between how the muscles feel when they are tensed and when they are relaxed. Then take a deep breath, hold it, and exhale slowly as you relax all your muscles, letting go of the tension. Notice the sense of relief as you relax. Now, go ahead and tense the individual groups of muscles one at a time. Hold the tension for a few seconds while you get a clear sense of what that feels like. Breathe deeply, hold your breath for a moment, and then let go of the tension as you exhale.

2) Form your hands into tight fists. Feel the tension through your hands and arms. Relax and let go of the tension. Now press your arms down against the surface they're resting on. Feel the tension. Hold it…and let go. Let your arms and hands go limp.

3) Shrug your shoulders tight, up toward your head, feeling the tension through your neck and shoulders. Hold, then gently release. Drop your shoulders down, free of tension.

4) Wrinkle your forehead, sensing the tightness. Hold…release, letting your forehead be smooth and relaxed. Shut your eyes as tight as you can. Hold…and let go. Now open your mouth as wide as you can. Hold it…gently relax, letting your lips touch softly. Then clench your jaw, teeth tight together. Hold…and relax. Let the muscles of your face be soft and relaxed, at ease.

5) Take a few moments to sense the relaxation throughout your arms and shoulders, up through your face. Now take a deep breath, filling your lungs down through your abdomen. Hold your breath while you feel the tension through your chest. Then exhale and let your chest relax with your breath, natural and easy. Suck in your stomach, holding the muscles tight…and relax. Arch your back, hold…and ease your back down gently, letting it relax. Feel the relaxation spread through your whole upper body.

6) Now tense your hips and buttocks, pressing your legs and heels against the surface beneath you. Hold…and relax. Curl your toes down, so they point away from your knees. Hold…and let go of the tension, relaxing your legs and feet. Then bend your toes back up towards your knees. Hold…and relax.

7) Now feel your whole body at rest, letting go of more tension with each breath: your face relaxed and soft…your arms and shoulders easy…your stomach, chest, and back soft and relaxed…your legs and feet resting at ease…your whole body soft and relaxed.

Take time to enjoy this state of relaxation for several minutes, feeling the deep calm and peace. When you're ready to get up, move slowly by sitting first and then gradually standing up.

Activities for the Soul: Enhancing Spirituality

Prayer

For some people, regular communication with their God is calming and reassuring. If your parent is accustomed to praying, or you think he or she would be willing to pray, suggest a couple of times a day that you each have a prayer, either silently or out loud. It can help both of you to refocus, especially when the events and responsibilities of the day seem to be overwhelming.

Breath Prayer

Another helpful kind of prayer is a breath prayer, a short, repeated prayer. If possible, you could teach this to your parent. If you do, be sure to let your parent choose his or her own prayer.

Taking Walks

Taking walks can enhance spirituality, as it is hard to look at nature and not feel some sense of awe at its beauty and perfection. Places you can walk with your parent or where you may let your parent walk alone if it is safe are:

- Parks
- Wooded areas
- Beaches
- Your own backyard

If it is not possible to take your parent outside, then take your walks inside with these options:

- **Use books** – Select books that show nature and its beauty.
- **Magazines** – Look through magazines together and point out what the beauty each of you sees.
- **Talk** – Talk your parent through a nature "walk", or if they can, let your parent talk you through a "walk."

Journal Writing

Your parent can benefit from keeping a journal. If your parent cannot write, let him or her tell you what to record from the day (or you may even be able to teach them to create an audio recording of themselves each day). If he or she can write, encourage a set time each day (maybe while you need to be attending to another responsibility) that or she sits with paper and pen and writes down whatever comes to mind. Encourage your parent to write about their feelings and emotions, if possible. Let your parent choose whether to share these writings with you; it is a personal possession to do with as he or she wishes.

Attending the Arts

Attending the arts in any form can be spiritually enhancing. The beauty of the human spirit and the talent that some people are gifted with can be uplifting and renewing. If you can, take your parent to:

- The art museum
- Theater, playhouses, or local schools or churches that frequently have wonderful productions (these community events are excellent options if either the cost or the crowds of the larger theater productions cause a problem)
- Musical productions, symphonies, operas, classical pop concerts, and ballet. Again, you can find local schools and churches that also have concerts if that makes things easier.

If your parent is unable or unwilling to leave the home, you can still experience the arts through:

- CDs or tapes, or play your own instrument.
- Pictures of art or reviews of plays.
- Virtual museum tours (*these have become increasingly popular during and after the 2020 pandemic*).
- Streaming concerts and events you can watch from home.
- Online art or music classes. If you saved programs of events you attended in the past, talk about them with your parent.

Encourage Service to Others

It's natural for us to want to feel useful and to have the ability to contribute in a meaningful way to help others. This sense of purpose and being needed is an important part of the human experience. It can enhance our overall well-being and cultivate a more wholesome and fulfilling outlook on life. Reaching out to help and support those around us taps into our innate desire to make a difference, which in turn can lead to greater happiness and life satisfaction. Serving others also eliminates and reduces isolation.

Consider asking your parent to do the following things for you:
- Fold laundry
- Clip coupons
- Set the table
- Do small repairs
- Anything else you can think of that they can do.

If your parent can do more, maybe he or she could:
- Volunteer to be a friendly phone visitor for other shut-ins.
- Send cards to people who are ill (*you can often obtain lists from a church, synagogue, or senior center and there are even multiple websites and organizations where you can send handwritten letters as an act of service – a simple online search will return multiple options*).
- Make gifts for the needy.

There are also numerous websites that provide ideas for how to serve and volunteer with local, national, in-person, virtual, full-time, and part-time options. A simple online search will provide a variety of options, and these websites may also prove a good starting point:
- *www.volunteermatch.org/*
- *www.justserve.org/*
- *www.idealist.org/en/*
- *www.allforgood.org/*

Participate in Activities

Social isolation can be particularly damaging for your parent, so it's important to help them find activities they enjoy and can participate in. These may be in-person activities such as:

- Places of worship
- Social clubs or senior centers
- Neighborhood gatherings

If your parent lives in a mobile home park or senior residence, there may be daily or weekly activities for them to participate in.

Technology has also expanded the opportunities to connect with others, so activities may also include participation in social media, video calls (*whether with a group or individual*), online forums, and other online events.

Look for Things to Laugh About

Keeping a sense of humor is healthy for both of you. Think about:

- Funny things you shared in the past.
- Some of the amusing events you are both experiencing in the present.
- Funny stories you can find online or books you can read together.
- Practice laughing! Not only is it good for your lungs and attitude, it's also a great way to spend the day with your loved one. Remember, laughter IS the best medicine!

11

Caregiver Resources

Caregivers often feel like they are floating in a sea of confusion and don't know where to turn or who to call to get the help they need. However, they cannot be effective without help. This chapter will give you ideas of where to go or who to call to get some help, whether you are caring for your parent, yourself, or directing other caregivers.

- Geriatric Care Managers
- Area Agency on Aging
- Day and Temporary Help
- Adult Day Health Care
- Hospice
- Transportation
- Emergency Response System
- Medical Supplies and Equipment
- Incontinence Supplies
- Food, Meals, and Groceries
- Medical Bill Paying Services
- Self-Help and Support Groups
- Blocking Junk Mail/Phone Calls
- Aging Organizations
- Phone Numbers for Free Health Information
- State-By-State Agencies on Aging
- State-By-State Insurance Departments

Geriatric Care Managers - (Aging Life Care Professional)

This is a very helpful resource, especially if you do not live in your parent's community or if your lifestyle cannot easily incorporate the day-to-day management of your parent's care.

The geriatric care manager is a professional who specializes in assisting older people and their families with care arrangements. Most geriatric care managers have substantial training in gerontology, social work, nursing, or counseling. They are competent to help you assist your aging parent in any of the following areas:

- Conduct care-planning assessments to identify problems and need for services.
- Screen, arrange, and monitor in-home help or other services.
- Review financial, legal, and medical issues, and offer referrals to appropriate geriatric specialists within these arenas.
- Provide crisis intervention.
- Act as a liaison to families at a distance, making sure things are going well and alerting families when their parent has a problem.
- Assist with moving an aging parent to or from a retirement complex, care home, or nursing home.
- The geriatric care manager can be your eyes, ears, and hands as you oversee the care of your parent. For more information on finding a Geriatric Care Manager (Aging Life Professional), call 1-520-881-8008 or go on their website at *https://www.aginglifecare.org/*

Area Agency on Aging

The Area Agency on Aging is a private, nonprofit organization that receives federal funds from the Older Americans Act, the Social Service Block Grants, and the United States Department of Agriculture. They also receive state appropriations.

To learn what this agency provides for the community in which your parent lives, call this **toll-free number: (800) 677-1116**. They will provide the phone number for your parent's local Area Agency on Aging. If the community is too small for an Area Agency on Aging office, there will be an office in a nearby larger community that serves your parent's community.

This organization fulfills a variety of roles, providing some direct support services while also overseeing and coordinating with other established programs catered towards the aging community. One of the direct services the Area Agency on Aging provides in most areas is the Senior Help Line. You or your parent can call the Senior Help Line to speak with specialists who are available to provide information and assistance about issues, services, and programs for seniors.

There are so many services and so much information available through this agency that it is a good resource to help you locate some of the services we suggest in the next few pages.

Your first call when you begin to look for resources should be to the Area Agency on Aging.

NOTE: Call the Eldercare Locator
(*Sponsored by the Area Agency on Aging national office*)
Toll-free 1-800-677-1116

Day and Temporary Help

If your completed assessment in Chapter Two indicates your parent can remain at home but needs a little help, you will need to hire someone to assist your parent. Based on the "Functional Assessment," you will know which areas your parent needs assistance in.

There are a variety of tasks and jobs that you can hire people to help with, including but not limited to the following:

- Companion-no "hands-on" work
- Assistance with bathing, dressing, and hair washing
- Assistance with toileting
- Housework
- Laundry and ironing
- Shopping
- Cooking
- Other errands, such as picking up prescriptions and transportation to appointments

Be sure you specify what tasks you expect to have done. You can arrange in-home help in whatever amount of time you feel is needed.

Most agencies will expect you to pay for a minimum of 3-4 hours at a time. You can hire help just for night-time or you can arrange for 24-hour per day help (normally in two 12-hour shifts or three 8-hour shifts.)

Unless your parent has a long-term care insurance policy that specifically states that it pays for "in-home help," your parent or the family will pay for these services out of pocket. This may be the time to determine if your parent is eligible for Medicaid or any other state, county, or city subsidized programs.

To locate the type of agency or programs that can assist in the home, contact your local Area Agency on Aging or the Department of Social Services in your parent's state.

1) This would be a good time to hire a geriatric care manager (Aging Life Care Professional) who will have a better working knowledge of the reliable resources that provide in-home assistance in your parent's community.
2) If you are hiring without the benefit of a professional geriatric care manager, please refer to <u>Chapter 5 - Options for Living Arrangements</u> *"What to Look for When Choosing In-Home Assistance for Your Parent,"* or look on the internet for Home Care Service Agencies.
3) If your parent is a member of a church, sometimes the pastor knows people in the church community who need of employment. That could be a benefit for both parties.

Adult Day Health Care

Adult Day Health Care (ADHC) offers care and supervised activities during the day for seniors and adults with disabilities. The programs are designed to meet the personal, health, rehabilitative, and social needs of your aging parent.

- For new clients, an application and screening process is required. That allows the professional staff to obtain information directly from you and your parent as well as from your parent's physician.
- Adult day care can be available for full days or partial days and from one to five days a week. The cost varies, and sometimes scholarships are available to offset some of the expense. Check your parent's long-term care insurance to see if it covers adult day health care (ADHC). Often these programs are subsidized by federal, county, or state funds.

Contact your parent's local Area Agency on Aging or Medicaid office to get a list of these centers. Hospital or Home Health social service staff could also provide you with this information.

If you are unable to obtain a local number, contact the Eldercare Locator and/or the National Council on Aging.

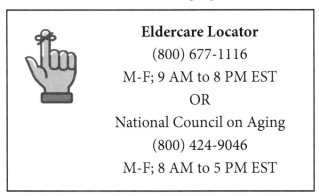

Eldercare Locator
(800) 677-1116
M-F; 9 AM to 8 PM EST
OR
National Council on Aging
(800) 424-9046
M-F; 8 AM to 5 PM EST

Hospice

Hospice is a philosophy that says: As people have a right to live with dignity, they also have a right to die with dignity.

Hospice is a special way of caring for people with terminal illnesses. The focus is on care not on cure. Hospice programs can provide care to the terminally ill person in their own home. Hospice is staffed by professional medical personnel who are trained in providing comfort care and relief from pain. This staff also offers help and support to the family members who are caring for the terminally ill person. Most hospices also have inpatient support available if it is needed.

If a terminally ill patient is covered by Medicare "Part A", they will automatically have the hospice benefit. The hospice benefit pays for most services related to the terminal illness if:

1) The patient's physician and the hospice medical director certify that the patient has a limited life expectancy (generally six months or less).
2) The patient chooses hospice care.
3) Care is provided by a hospice program certified by Medicare.

If your parent's physician believes your parent is in the end stage of his life, he will probably talk to you about hospice or he may ask a social worker or nurse to educate you about the hospice programs in your parent's area.

The information in this workbook gives you an overview of what hospice is so you will have some familiarity with it.

- You can also call a local hospice program or you can talk to a medical social worker at your parent's local hospital, home health agency, or outpatient clinic affiliated with your parent's local hospital.
- We recommend that you become acquainted and knowledgeable about this alternate medical care approach before your parent is in a terminal illness crisis.

For more information about hospice, contact these organizations:

- **National Hospice and Palliative Care Organization**
  1731 King Street, Alexandria, VA 22314
  (703) 837-1500
  https://www.nhpco.org/
- **National Association of Home Care & Hospice**
  202-547-7424
  https://www.nahc.org/
- **Visiting Nurse Associations of America (VNAA)**
  202-508-9498
  http://www.vnaa.org
- **Hospice Foundation of America (HFA)**
  1-800-854-3402
  www. hospicefoundation.org
- **For Cancer Information Service call 1-800-4-cancer**
  (1-800-422-6237)

Transportation

Getting your parent from one location to another can be a problem. Some communities have better resources than others. The following are suggestions that you may explore.

Parent's Car - If your parent owns a car and can afford to keep the insurance and registration current, you can make arrangements with a neighbor or friend to drive your parent in his or her own car. Be sure the designated driver has a valid driver's license.

Americans with Disabilities Act (ADA) - The ADA is a federal law that mandates equal opportunity for the disabled (including the elderly) in many areas, one of which is transportation.

- Specialized transportation must be provided for people who are unable to use city buses. In most cities, this transportation is operated by the city via Dial-a-Ride.
- Look online for Dial-a-Ride or its equivalent. You will need to request an application for the Americans with Disabilities Act for transportation.
- The cost for ADA transportation will be minimal – check with the Dial-a-Ride for current costs.
- **Handicap Transport Service** - These services are privately owned. They offer several means of transport which include wheelchair vans, stretcher vans, or ambulances. Locate their phone numbers under "Ambulance Service" via web search.

American Red Cross - An American Red Cross service is available for transportation, but only for medical-related appointments.

American Cancer Society - If your parent's community has an American Cancer Society, they may provide transportation for cancer treatments and related medical appointments.

Volunteer Organizations - Sometimes churches or other service-minded organizations can provide transportation for their communities. A call to a local church might direct you to that service if it exists.

Private Transportation Services - There are some private services just for elderly and handicapped people. The cost is generally less than a taxi but more than the public forms of transportation. If such a service exists in your parent's community, you might find a phone number online.

Local Hospital - Some hospitals maintain a van for the transportation of their patients who need visits to outpatient or rehabilitation clinics or for radiation or other medical-related appointments on the hospital campus. A call to the hospital will give you the information you need.

Geriatric Care Manager (Aging Life Care Professional) - For help arranging and coordinating transportation, consult with a geriatric care manager. For a fee, this professional will consult with you regarding what type of transportation services are available in your parent's community.

To locate a geriatric care manager in your area, call the Aging Life Care Association at (520) 881-8008.

Emergency Response System

No matter how many phones are in the home, if your parent falls or has a medical emergency away from a phone, he or she may not be able to reach it to summon help. An emergency response system is a means by which your parent can summon help without using the telephone.

An emergency response system has a lightweight, waterproof medallion with a remote-control button that your parent wears, either as a necklace or a wristband. A push of the button activates a small in-home unit that automatically puts your parent in touch with a monitoring company. The company will follow the instructions you have provided should your parent need immediate help.

Many companies sell or rent emergency response systems. Renting is generally the most cost-effective. You should be able to rent the equipment and service for around $30-$60 a month.

To locate one of these companies:
1) Call the local hospital and ask to speak with a social worker. That person will be knowledgeable about what is available in your parent's community.
2) If your area has an information and referral service for community resources, this is also a good way to locate this equipment. (Area Agency on Aging in your area can also assist: some agencies have a Senior Help Line—this is a very important phone number to obtain from this agency – BE SURE TO RECORD this as an important phone number).
3) Call your parent's local Area Agency on Aging to see if they can guide you in locating this service: (800) 677-1116 (Elder Locators).

Medical Supplies Equipment

Since there are limits to what Medicare will provide, you may find yourself in need of some equipment not covered by your parent's insurance. Here are a few ideas on how to obtain that equipment:

- Some supplies and equipment may be available at no cost through organizations like the American Cancer Society or the Easter Seal Society.
- Some communities may have loan closets, which are not related to specific illnesses, such as the Salvation Army or churches. Each place you call, ask for locations and phone numbers of other loan closets.
- If your parent lives in a mobile home park or other senior housing community, the manager may be aware of equipment available for loan or sale.
- Medical supply stores will carry most equipment and might have used equipment.

Incontinence Supplies

Keeping your parent dry with no skin breakdown can be difficult. There are a variety of incontinence products available, such as adult diapers, pull-ups, pant liners, and pads for their chairs and bed. You can purchase these products at pharmacies and medical supply stores, as well as in department stores, grocery stores, and drug stores. Coupons are often available in magazines or online such as AARP's Modern Maturity.

Food, Meals, and Groceries

Getting meals or food can be difficult for someone who cannot drive and/or cook. If your assessment indicates your parent could stay at home with some help with meal preparation or shopping, then you will want to explore the following:

- **Area Agency on Aging** - If your parent needs a meal service program but you are unable to locate one, contact the Area Agency on Aging at (800) 677-1116. They will be able to direct you to the meal service within your parent's community. Another option is to call your parent's local community information and referral service helpline.

- **Geriatric Care Managers** - For a fee, a geriatric care manager will help you locate and coordinate meal services for your aging parent. To locate a geriatric care manager in your area, call the Aging Life Care Association at (520) 881-8008.

- **Hospital Meals** - Some hospitals have a meal delivery service within a set boundary. You may be able to arrange the purchase and delivery of a daily meal from there. If that is available to your parent, you will probably need to contact his/her doctor for a referral.

- **Meals on Wheels** - These may be delivered from senior centers, churches, or other volunteer organizations. Each community organizes the delivery of meals in its own way. Call the local hospital and ask to speak to a social worker. She or he will be knowledgeable about most of the community services.

- **Schwan's Home Delivery/Yelloh This** - A well-established frozen food delivery company with an extensive menu including all but fresh dairy and produce. (888) 724-9267 *https://www.yelloh.com/*
- **Groceries Online** - You can look up grocery stores where your parent shops that offer online purchases and delivery options.

Medical Bill Paying Services

The frustrations and challenges that come with understanding and paying the medical bills following an illness can be the undoing of your parent or the caregiver. Some communities have services that specialize in analyzing and organizing medical bill information and informing you of exactly what needs to be paid and to whom. They will keep you informed when deductibles are met and will challenge requests for money that didn't get billed to the secondary insurance. There can be a monthly fee established with extra services billed separately or the service may charge separately for each bill they handle. You may want to discuss the service and charges with one or more bill-paying services.

It is often difficult to locate these services since they frequently don't advertise. Most of their clients come through referrals from:
- Elder Law attorneys
- Geriatric care managers (Aging Life Professionals)
- Social workers
- Courts
- Certified public accountants
- Fiduciaries

All these referral sources can be located by web search. Call any of them and ask for the names and phone numbers of at least two medical bill-paying services.

Most geriatric care managers are already working with one of these bill-paying services. To locate a geriatric care manager in your area, call the Aging Life Care Association at (520) 881-8008.

Self-Help and Support Groups

It is estimated that 15 million people each year look for help and support among others who face a common problem. Participants of self-help and support groups share their experiences, knowledge, and coping ideas with each other. These groups can be small and meet in a member's home or they can be quite large and meet in rented or donated locations. Some groups are part of a national organization that sends out newsletters and updated information on whatever their mission is. Other groups are local only and develop their own mailings if needed.

Generally, there are no fees charged, but often donations are asked if any costs are incurred. If speakers are brought in to share information or do a special program, admission may be charged. Most groups welcome any new members and are available to reach out to those sharing a common problem.

Support groups usually meet once a month; however, that will depend on the needs and desires of the group. Although it will require time and effort on your part to be available to meet with your support group, it is beneficial for you to do so. Even if you must drive to a nearby community to find a group that supports your needs, the benefits will likely outweigh the inconvenience. Caregiver support groups are particularly advantageous if you have the primary responsibility of caring for your parent.

To locate a group, whether it is for caregivers or support about a specific illness or problem, call the Area Agency on Aging at 1-800-677-1116, and ask for their phone number in your state. The local agency will have a Community Information & Referral Help Line that you can call to ask about self-help and support groups.

Blocking Junk Mail/Phone Calls

You may notice that an inordinate number of catalogs, lottery solicitations, magazine subscription requests, etc., are being delivered to your parent's home. The Direct Marketing Association is a trade group that represents many of the businesses that utilize the mail to solicit customers. A letter to the following address requesting them to discontinue advertising mail to your parent's name and address will help decrease the number of mailings. Since they can only control the companies they represent, your parent may still receive unwanted pieces of advertising. It takes about three months for the request to take effect.

Mail Preference Service Direct Marketing Service
P.O. Box 9008
Farmingdale, NY 11735

It is also possible to curtail the number of telemarketing calls placed to your parent's phone number. If you wish to do that you may write to the following address. You can request that they discontinue all telemarketing calls to the phone number you give them.

Telephone Preference Service Direct Marketing Association
P.O. Box 9014
Farmingdale, NY 11735

Aging Organizations

1) **AARP**
   AARP is a nonprofit membership organization dedicated to addressing the needs and interests of persons 50 and older. Their site provides useful information and resources on topics, such as health and wellness, economic security, work, long-term care, independent living, and personal enrichment. http://www.aarp.org

2) **American Society on Aging**
   The American Society on Aging is a nonprofit organization committed to enhancing the knowledge and skills of those working with older adults and their families. Their site offers useful resources on a variety of aging-related topics. http://www.asaging.org

3) **National Council on Aging (NCOA)**
   So many of us, whether we realize it or not, are caregivers. Approximately 40 million Americans provide unpaid care to older adults and adults with disabilities—the majority of whom also juggle a job or other responsibilities. Wearing all these hats can take its toll. Let NCOA be there for you. https://www.ncoa.org/caregivers

Phone Numbers for Free Health Information

This is a list of toll-free numbers of organizations that provide health-related information.

National Area Agency on Aging   **(800) 677-1116**
   Eldercare locators and other information and local referrals.

National Institute on Aging Information Center   **(800) 222-2225**
   Information about healthy aging. Provides literature and referrals to organizations dealing with specific age-related illnesses.

National Council on Aging   **(800) 424-9046**
   Information on family caregiving, senior employment, and long-term care.

American Diabetes Association   **(800) 342-2383**

Provides information and referrals to local support group assistance.

American Council of the Blind   **(800) 424-8666**

Information on blindness. Gives references to clinics, rehabilitation organizations, research centers, and local chapters. Publishes a resource list.

American Foundation for Urologic Disorders   **(800) 242-2383**

Provides written information and referrals for individuals with urological diseases.

American Council on Alcoholism   **(800) 527-5344**

Treatment referrals and counseling for recovering alcoholics and their families.

Hear Now   **(800) 328-8602**

Distributes reconditioned hearing aids. Provides services for hearing-impaired who do not have financial resources to purchase hearing aids.

Dial-A-Hearing Screening Test   **(800) 222-3277**

Answers questions on hearing problems and provides referrals to local numbers for a two-minute hearing test. Provides referrals to organizations with information on hearing problems.

Medicare Information Line   **(800) 633-4227**

Gives information on Medicare issues and Medigap insurance.

Social Security Office   **(800) 772-1213**

Information about Social Security benefits and supplement security income. Referrals are made to your parent's local Social Security office.

National Alliance on Mental Illness (NAMI)   **(800) 950-6264**

Free literature about depression effective treatments, and referrals to physicians. (301) 443-4513.

National Foundation for Depressive Illness
Describes symptoms of depression and offers information and physician referrals.

Cancer Information Service   **(800) 422-6237**
Answers questions from cancer patients, their families, and the public.

Lung Line Information Service   **(800) 222-5864**
Information about asthma, emphysema, chronic bronchitis, allergies, and respiratory system disorders.

Arthritis Foundation Information Line   **(800) 283-7800**
Provides information on arthritis and referrals to local chapters.

Alzheimer's Association   **(800) 272-3900**
Provides referrals to local chapters and support groups. Publications are available.

State-by-State Agencies on Aging
The agencies on aging are responsible for coordinating services for older Americans. Here is a list of those agencies by state.

Alabama
Commission on Aging
1-800-AGE-LINE   (1-800-243-5463)

Alaska
Older Alaskans Commission   (907) 465-3250

Arizona
Department of Economic Security: Aging and Adult Administration
(602) 542-4446

Arkansas
Division of Aging and Adult Services (501) 682-2441

California
Department of Aging   (916) 419-7591

Colorado
Aging and Adult Services: Department of Social Services (303) 866-2800

Connecticut
Elderly Services Division   (800) 994-9422

Delaware
Division of Aging: Department of Health and Social Services
1-800-223-9074

District of Columbia
Office on Aging   (202) 724-5626 or (202) 724-5622

Florida
Department of Elder Affairs   (850) 414-2060 or (800) 96ELDER

Georgia
Division of Aging Services: Department of Human Resources
(404) 657 -5258

Hawaii
Executive Office on Aging   (808) 586-0100

Idaho
Office on Aging   (208) 334-3833

Illinois
Department on Aging   (800) 252-8966

Indiana
Division of Aging and Home Services
(317) 232- 7020 or (800) 545-7763

Iowa
Department of Elder Affairs   (515) 725-3333

Kansas
Department on Aging   (785) 296-4986

Kentucky
Division of Aging Services: Cabinet for Human Resources
(502) 564-6930

Louisiana
Governor's Office of Elderly Affairs   (225) 342-7100

Maine
State of Maine Office of Aging & Disability Services (207) 287-3707

Maryland
Office on Aging   (410) 767-0708

Massachusetts
Executive Office of Elder Affairs   (617) 727-7750 or (800) 882-2003

Michigan
Office of Services to the Aging   (517) 241-4100

Minnesota
Board on Aging   (651) 431-2500

Mississippi
Division of Aging and Adult Services   1-800-345-6347

Missouri
Division of Aging: Department of Social Services   (573) 526-4542

Montana
Office on Aging: Department of Public Health and Human Services
(406) 444-7784

Nebraska
Department on Aging   (402) 471-2307

Nevada
Department of Human Resources: Division for Aging Services
(702) 486-3545

New Hampshire
Department of Health and Human Services: Division of Elderly and Adult
Services   (603) 271- 4680

New Jersey
Department of Community Affairs: Division on Aging
(908) 475-6591 or (877) 222- 3737

New Mexico
State Agency on Aging   (505) 827-7640

New York
State Office for the Aging   (800) 342-9871

North Carolina
Division of Aging   (919) 855-3400

North Dakota
Department of Human Services: Aging Services Division   (701) 328-8910

Ohio
Department of Aging   (614) 466 1221 or (800) 282-1206

Oklahoma
Department of Human Services: Aging Service Division
(405) 521-2281

Oregon
Department of Human Resources: Senior and Disabled Services Division
(503) 945-5811

Pennsylvania
Department of Aging: "APPRISE" Health Insurance Counseling and
Assistance   (800) 783- 7067

Puerto Rico
Governor's Office of Elderly Affairs: Gericulture Commission
(787) 721-6121

Rhode Island
Department of Elderly Affairs   (401) 462-3000

South Carolina
Division on Aging   (803) 898-2850

South Dakota
Office of Adult Services and Aging   (605) 773-5990

Tennessee
Commission on Aging   (615) 741-2056

Texas
Department on Aging   (800) 252-9240

Utah
Utah Commission on Aging   (801) 213-4156

Vermont
Department of Aging and Disabilities (802) 241-2401

Virginia
Department for the Aging   (804) 662-9333 or (800) 552-3402

Washington
Commission of Aging   (301) 790-0275

West Virginia
Commission on Aging   (304) 558-3317

Wisconsin
Wisconsin Department of Health Services   (608) 266-1865

Wyoming
Division on Aging   (307) 777- 7995

The national number for locating the Area Agency on Aging in your parent's community is **(800) 677-1116.**

State-by-State Insurance Departments

Every state has laws and regulations governing all types of insurance. Below is a list of all the state insurance departments that are responsible for enforcing these laws and providing the public with insurance information.

Alabama
Insurance Department: Consumer Service Division   (334) 269-3550

Alaska
Division of Insurance   (907) 465 2515

American Samoa
Insurance Department: Office of the Governor   (684) 633-4116

Arizona
Insurance Department   (602) 364-3100

Arkansas
Insurance Department: Seniors Insurance Network   (501) 371-2782

California
Department of Insurance   (213) 897-8921 or (800) 927-4357

Colorado
Insurance Division   (303) 894-7499 ext. 0 or (800) 930-3745

Connecticut
Insurance Department   (860) 297-3800 or (800) 203-3447

Delaware
Insurance Department   (302) 674-7300 or (800) 282-8611

District of Columbia
Insurance Department: Consumer and Professional Services Bureau
(202) 727-8000

Florida
Department of Insurance   (850) 413-3140

Georgia
Insurance Department   (404) 656-2056

Hawaii
Department of commerce and Consumer Affairs: Insurance Division
(808) 586-2790

Idaho
Insurance Department: SHIBA Program   (208) 334-4350

Illinois
Insurance Department   (217) 782-4515

Indiana
Insurance Department   (317) 232-2395 or (800) 622-4461

Iowa
Insurance Division   (515) 281- 5705

Kansas
Insurance Department   (785) 296-3071

Kentucky
Insurance Department   (502) 564-3630

Louisiana
Department of Insurance   (225) 342-5900

Maine
Bureau of Insurance   (207) 624- 8475

Maryland
Insurance Administration Complaints and Investigations Unit: Life and
Health   (410) 468-2244 or (800) 492-6116

Massachusetts
Insurance Division: Consumer Services Section   (877) 563-4467

Michigan
Insurance Bureau   (517) 284-8800 or (517)-284-8837
                     (877) 999-6442

Minnesota
Insurance Department: Department of Commerce
(651) 539-1500 or (800) 657-3602

Mississippi
Insurance Department: Consumer Assistance Division   (601) 359- 3569

Missouri
Department of Insurance: Consumer Assistance Division
(573) 751-2640 or (800) 726-7390

Montana
Insurance Department (Life and Health)   (406) 444-2040

Nebraska
Insurance Department   (402) 471-2201

Nevada
Department of Business and Industry: Division of Insurance
Las Vegas - (702) 486-4009
Carson City - (775) 687-0700

New Hampshire
Insurance Department: Life and Health Division
(603) 271-2261 or (800) 852-3416

New Jersey
Insurance Department   (800) 446-7467

New Mexico
Insurance Department   (505) 827-4601

New York
Insurance Department   (212) 480-6400 or (800) 342-3736

North Carolina
Insurance Department: Seniors' Health Insurance Information Program
(SHIP)   (855) 408-1212

North Dakota
Insurance Department   (701) 328-2440 or (800) 247-0560

Ohio
Insurance Department: Consumer Services Division
(614) 644-2673 or (800) 686-1526

Oklahoma
Insurance Department   (405) 521-6628

Oregon
Department of Consumer and Business Services: Senior Health Insurance
Benefit Assistance   (800) 722-4134

Pennsylvania
Insurance Department: consumer Service Bureau   (717) 787-2317

Rhode Island
Insurance Division   (401) 462-9500

South Carolina
Department of Insurance: Consumer Affairs Section
(803) 737 6180 or (800) 768-3467

South Dakota
Insurance Department   (605) 773-3563

Tennessee
Department of Commerce and Insurance: Insurance Assistance Office
(615) 741-2241

Texas
Department of Insurance Complaints Resolution
(512) 676-6500 or (800) 252-3439

Utah
Insurance Department: Consumer Services   (801) 538-3805

Vermont
Department of Banking and Insurance: Consumer Complaint Division
(802) 828-3302

Virginia
Bureau of Insurance   (804) 371-9691 or (800) 552-7945

Washington
Insurance Department   (360) 753- 7300 or (800) 562-6900

West Virginia
Insurance Department: Consumer Services   (304) 558- 3386

Wisconsin
Insurance Department: Complaints Department
(608) 266-0103 or (800) 236-8517

Wyoming
Insurance Department   (307) 777-7401

ACKNOWLEDGMENTS

I would like to express my sincere gratitude to the many people who provided encouragement, feedback, and support throughout the publishing process of this book.

I would first like to thank Sandra Portney, my attorney, who was instrumental in supporting and encouraging me to write this book.

A special thanks to Sylvia Post, Brent Owens, and Jim Davidson who also encouraged me to write this book.

I thank the staff at A.G.E. Consultants, Inc.; Marilyn Heinrichs, Marie Eid, Sylvia Washington, and Julie Nitzkin who shared their knowledge and dedication to providing the best care for our geriatric clients.

I would like to acknowledge Gina Mercer, Candace Silva, and Greg Novak who took the time to read this book to give me feedback on the contents.

Thanks to Patti Hultstrand, Margaret Grady, and Donna Stark who prepared this book for publication.

Finally, I would like to thank all the wonderful clients and their families who allowed me to assist in providing care for them.

For More Information Contact:
Barbara Applegate, MSW, ACSW
A.G.E. Consultants
7320 N. Dreamy Draw Dr.
Phoenix, AZ 85020
Phone: (602) 331-8105

Made in the USA
Columbia, SC
05 March 2025

54723219R00157